Earthwalks
for Body and Spirit

**Exercises to Restore Our Sacred
Bond with the Earth**

JAMES ENDREDY

**Foreword by
VICTOR SANCHEZ**

Bear & Company
Rochester, Vermont

Bear & Company
One Park Street
Rochester, Vermont 05767
www.InnerTraditions.com

Library of Congress Cataloging-in-Publication Data

Endredy, James.
    Earthwalks for body and spirit : exercises to restore our sacred bond with the earth / James Endredy ; foreword by Victor Sanchez.
        p. cm.
    ISBN 1-879181-78-9 (pbk.)
    1. Walking. 2. Meditation. 3. Nature—Religious aspects. 4. Human ecology—Religious aspects. I. Title.
    GV199.5 .E53 2002
    796.51—dc21   20022000065

Printed and bound in Canada

10 9 8 7 6 5 4 3 2 1

Text design and layout by Priscilla Baker
This book was typeset in Caslon, with Caslon Antique and Gill Sans used as display typefaces

Dedicated to my father, Jenö Endrédy,
and my mother, Irma Endrédy

Contents

Acknowledgments

Without the love and support of many people, this book would not have materialized.

Thanks to my brothers Victor Sanchez, Manolo Cetina, Armando Cruz, Demian Ortiz, and Alberto Trevino for all their efforts and continued support of my personal growth and projects.

Thanks to Jody Spehar for her advice and expertise in the publishing world, and for her friendship and golden heart.

Thanks to my wonderfully talented editor, Elaine Sanborn, and to everyone else at Inner Traditions • Bear & Company.

Special thanks to Joyce and Ed Calvitti, who fed, housed, and nurtured me and provided unfailing support and critical insight during months of writing, and to all the others who helped and encouraged me during the writing, including: Barbara Gross; Mark, Mark Jr., and Karen Beatty; Cindy and Jerry Leahy; Sue Kligerman; and my mom and sister, Irma and Cindy Endredy.

Thanks to my one and only Arankanéni.

Thanks to all the people throughout the world who have shared the magic of my activities in the Art of Living Purposefully—you walk with me always.

Thanks to my Huichol Elders and brothers and sisters for opening their hearts and homes so that I could glimpse their ancient and powerful tradition.

There are no words to acknowledge my brother and sister deer that guide my way.

And last, I want to acknowledge the three things that have kept my heart beating for the last few years: my visions in Aquel Lugar, my grandfather Tatewari, and of course my best buddy, Aragorn, the Wonder Dog.

Foreword

I met Jim Endredy years ago in Mexico, during my first AVP*
workshop for English speakers called "The Jump to the Other
Self." He was part of a group of people whose members had traveled to Mexico from different countries, mostly from the United
States. My work consisted of helping them bring their spiritual
quest down to earth through a series of exercises based on the
following basic principles:

• What draws people to a spiritual quest is their longing for
  a transcendental experience, a desire to reconnect with the
  ultimate source of everything that exists: the Great Spirit.

• Human awareness comprehends an essential duality made
  up of what the ancient indigenous people from Mexico
  called *tonal* (based on reason) and *nagual* (based on silent

*AVP is the Spanish acronym for El Arte de Vivir a Proposito or, in English,
the Art of Living Purposefully. It is the organization created by Victor Sanchez
for personal and spiritual growth. One of its main influences is the knowledge
of the Toltecs. AVP works to carry this knowledge to others through, in part,
translating Toltec practices and perspectives to fit with the needs and circumstances of people in our modern society. AVP conducts workshops worldwide
that are centered on recovering awareness of the other self and sharing the
hidden treasures of indigenous knowledge.

knowledge). The two sides of this duality can also be called the *self* and *the other self*.

- The transcendental experience of reconnecting with the Great Spirit takes place beyond the self and can only be achieved through entering the realm of the other self.

- To enter the realm of the other self and from there, to reconnect with the Great Spirit, no intermediaries are required. What is necessary, however, is that we take personal responsibility for the journey, look for well founded information, being creative, and develop a sensible series of concrete practices.

Common to esoteric and New Age thinking is the belief that the key to a successful spiritual quest is in finding the right teacher or guide. But when we focus too much on someone else's apparent power and stop using our own criteria, we may fall into the trap of looking outside of ourselves for what can only be found inside. This infantile tendency to depend upon "illuminated masters" is something that must be left behind if we are seriously committed to finding our own path.

Two of the key aspects of the "Jump to the Other Self" experience is that you jump by yourself, with only your soul to accompany you; and that your solitary action of jumping into the mystery is all that you have in that moment.

It is through this jump, both metaphorical and real, that you recover your inner vision and discover that there is another self living within your being—the other self, which is magical and apprehends the world through silent knowledge and provides the meaning and direction for your everyday life.

This was what Jim and his fellow participants in that special group had come to discover in Mexico. Fortunately, most of them were ready to face the simple truth: If they wanted to jump to the other self, they would have to make it on their own.

And jump they did! That first group of foreigners traveling so far to learn was very special to me because its members helped me to keep learning that despite nationality, language, religion, or age, we are all the same inside.

During that first workshop, Jim's focus and effort were remarkable. But only in the following years could I see the magnitude of his commitment to the task of *being*.

To that end, Jim started traveling to Mexico for advanced workshops—we worked together in the mountains of Michoacán and the jungle of Chiapas, by the ocean and in the desert—and through his commitment he found a place for himself in our relationship and work with the Wirrarika people, an indigenous group whom we call the surviving Toltecs.

Everyone in our group was amazed at Jim's efforts at home in the United States to earn the money and time to travel frequently to Mexico. In fact, he participated so often in our work that it seemed as though he lived in our country full-time. As a natural consequence of his commitment and care he became, in record time, a very professional and capable AVP instructor—and our first non-Mexican instructor, at that.

During that time, he managed to open his own avenues for further development of his connection with the Wirrarika. From at first just listening to our stories of the world of the surviving Toltecs, he came to the point when he was telling us his own stories from that same world.

I remember one in particular:

Jim had once visited a specific Wirrarika village, looking for an indigenous friend who would accompany him to the core ceremonial center in another remote village of the Sierra Madres. Interestingly enough, he didn't find the person he was looking for but instead made friends with a group of Indians from that community—just like that, with no apparent effort. Soon he was offered a place to stay in one of their humble homes, and was sharing meals with them in a world where food supplies are very limited and a simple bowl of beans and tortillas is a feast.

But how had he managed to be accepted so completely and so quickly by them?

Well, the answer was quite simple: He was there in their village simply as a human being among other human beings. While his original goal was to travel to the ceremonial center to look for spiritual experiences, he was not closed to the magic hidden behind the simple things of everyday life. Those Indians were simply working in their fields, preparing the land for the corn planting, and Jim simply asked if he could help them with their work.

At first they were not sure if the funny *gringo* was serious about his offer—to work just for the sake of helping. But Jim was carrying his machete and helped them for several full days of cleaning and preparing the land. It was hard work. After all this working and sweating with them, there existed a bond between the gringo and the Indians.

It turned out that among those villagers there were powerful and very wise *marakames** who were to become very important to Jim, though he didn't know it when he first began to spend time with them. Indeed, if he had focused only on looking for shamans, he certainly wouldn't have wasted his time with "simple peasants"! Only because his heart was open to the simple magic of human company could he grasp the invisible opportunity and find his way into that world. I still remember Jim's words:

"And do you know what, Vic? There were powerful marakames among them, but what impressed me most was not their shamanic power, which was great, but the amazing care and respect they

---

*A *marakame* is a healer and shaman who sings the voice of Grandfather Fire.

gave to every single thing they used or interacted with—whether it was their machetes, the seed, the land, the people around them, or a small campfire they lit for warmth in the cold night. It's as if every little thing is sacred to them. In our city world, where almost everything is treated as worthless, we don't understand that. We consume, we own objects that we throw away after a while. We use everything and everyone with no care and we waste without even thinking, while those people who have almost nothing use everything with care and respect. Oh man! We need to learn from those people. If only we could be just a little bit like them!"

I felt proud to be his friend when I heard Jim's words. I thought, *At least we have one person here who understands what the whole idea of learning from the Indians is about.*

How difficult it is for some people to see that real magic does not reside in the "supernatural powers" of shamans described in the pages of a book, but in the special way they deal with everyday life. It involves nothing too complicated: treating the world and each other with respect, talking to the Fire, touching Mother Earth with a profound feeling of communion in your heart.

In Jim, I knew, there was at least one man who had worked and walked long enough to see what so many others couldn't. And I was pleased that he was a true member of our spiritual family, sharing the same sacred task: helping people in the world to rescue the missing half of human awareness: the other self.

Earthwalks for Body and Spirit is a prime example of Jim's commitment to the task of what I call *shamanic technology,* which is the means not to become shamans but to make the shamanic shift of awareness—that is, to enter the magical side of our awareness where silent knowledge and connection with the Great Spirit are one and the same. I like *Earthwalks for Body and Spirit* because it is a practical book telling you not only what can be reached, but also how to get there. Using it, you can discover the magic behind conscious walking and open the door to your other self.

Learning to walk is learning to live. If you try to learn something new about walking each time you go for a walk, you will be learning about every part of your life. Walking rescues you from the limits of the past and the fantasy of the future and opens you to the present. In that present you cannot be alone, because you are always walking on *and with* the Earth. *She is alive* and talks to us continually in her own way. This book is about making this sacred connection as you walk so that your journey becomes a rite of passage into another world where reality is much more than what you have known and where you are able to discover unknown regions of your own soul.

The world needs such medicine. We are lucky that Jim has taken on the tasks of both designing and collecting these Earthwalks for all the walkers in the world.

—VICTOR SANCHEZ

Preface

Earthwalks for Body and Spirit was written as a result of a vision I experienced in a sacred and remote desert region of northern Mexico. I know from deep in my heart that the vision and message that prompted me to share my experiences in the form of this book came directly from Earth herself, for she is injured and is crying and calling out to me—to all of us.

Although my vision was not clear as to the exact contents of this book, the actual experience of writing it has been an extremely enlightening process. It has provided the realization that it is my experiences of walking and searching for the spiritual answers to my questions about the world and my life that have led me to this point—I have been guided to share with people the ways of walking Earth that have been shared with me.

Anyone who can see, listen, read, walk, or breathe knows Earth is crying from the injuries inflicted upon her by the human race, and each of us realizes and reacts to this in different ways and at different levels. For those of us who have been blessed with life experiences that have connected us to the world of Nature, this crying can be heard clearly and felt in the deepest regions of our being. Many people have responded to Earth's pain and have taken it upon themselves to offer their specific talents and knowledge to answer her call. This book is my contribution. My talents and knowledge are not in the realm of exact science, psychology, or ecology, but rather are a result of many years of walking in a way that maintains a connection to the natural powers and forces that guide Earth, life-altering events within the world of indigenous communities, and all that I have learned from sharing these themes with people in workshop settings.

This book is about walking outdoors in such a way that our attention is focused on the elements and activities of the natural world. By placing attention on these aspects of Nature that are foreign to our usual experiences in modern-day industrial culture, we create a rift in the continuity of the psychic numbness[*] that inhibits people from reacting to our current path of destruction of Earth. At the same time, Earthwalks cultivate deep experiences related to the amount of stimuli that the world of Nature provides, and they foster a connection to this world that we can establish once we intend to do so. These results, together with the physical movement required to attain them, can help to raise our quality of life and open our hearts to feeling the profound love of Earth. The wise words of D. H. Lawrence echo this theme:

> When we get out of the glass bottles of our ego, and when we escape like squirrels turning in the cages of our personality and get into the forests again, we shall shiver with cold and fright but things will happen to us so that we don't know ourselves. Cool, unlying life will rush in, and passion will make our bodies taut with power, we shall stamp our feet with new power and old things will fall down, we shall laugh, and institutions will curl up like burnt paper.[†]

---

[*]Laura Sewall, "The Skill of Ecological Perception," in Theodore Roszak, Mary E. Gomes, and Allen D. Kanner, eds., *Ecopsychology: Restoring the Earth, Healing the Mind* (San Francisco: Sierra Club Books, 1995).

[†]D. H. Lawrence in Elizabeth Powers and Elias Amidon, *Earth Prayers* (New York: HarperCollins, 1991).

BEAR CUB BOOKS

BEAR & CO.

Inner Traditions • Bear & Company

P.O. Box 388
Rochester, VT 05767-0388
U.S.A.

Please send us this card to receive our latest catalog.

❑ Check here if you would like to receive our catalog via e-mail.

E-mail address _____

Name _____ Company _____

Address _____

City _____ State _____ Zip _____ Phone _____ Country _____

Please check the following area(s) of interest to you:
❑ Health   ❑ Self-help   ❑ Spirituality   ❑ Shamanism
❑ Ancient Mysteries ❑ New Age   ❑ Tarot   ❑ Martial Arts
❑ Spanish Language   ❑ Sexuality/Drugs ❑ Children   ❑ Teen

Order at 1-800-246-8648 • Fax (802) 767-3726
E-mail: orders@InnerTraditions.com • Web site: www.InnerTraditions.com

Because modern culture promotes single-minded pursuits and is oriented toward the goal rather than the road taken to reach it, there are many magical aspects of Nature that we either take for granted or never even notice. Earthwalks combine the physical activity of walking with purposeful attention to Nature's magic. Darkness, reflection, wind, shadow, sunlight, water, balance, fire, scents, textures, and living beings—our relationship to each of these can be experienced and explored as we walk so that we can reconnect to the web of life of which we are a part and to which we so desperately need to return. As Albert Einstein eloquently said:

> A human being is part of the whole, called by us the universe. A part limited in time and space. He experiences himself, his thoughts and feelings, as something separate from the rest, a kind of optical delusion of his consciousness. This delusion is a kind of prison for us, restricting us to our personal desires and to affection for a few persons near to us. Our task must be to free ourselves from this prison by widening our circle of compassion to embrace all living creatures.*

Some have suggested that the techniques presented here are shamanic in origin. While this descriptive phrase is not inappropriate for the overall context of this book, please be aware that Earthwalks are intended to improve quality of life and promote Earth healing, not to create shamans. But there are distinct benefits to an awareness of the shamanic aspects of these walks, regardless of the words used to describe them. My personal interests in indigenous culture and shamanism have led me to relate to Nature in ways that have enabled me to move past the controlling side of my ego and connect with a wider view of reality. This has radically transformed my life into one filled with

---

*Albert Einstein, quoted in David Suzuki, *The Sacred Balance: Rediscovering Our Place in Nature* (Vancouver: Greystone Books, 1997).

more love and laughter. The word *shamanism* has myriad meanings these days and for the Earthwalks collected here the words of Dr. Leslie Gray seem appropriate:

> Shamanism is the oldest form of mind/body healing known to humankind . . . [it] is estimated to be at least forty thousand years old. It's been practiced perennially by virtually all indigenous peoples up to today. The worldview of shamanism is that health equals balanced relationships with all living things. When someone is ill, shamanism attempts to restore power to them by putting them back in harmony with life. This idea that all things are connected, while a very ancient concept, is also a concept for the future. At the dawn of the twenty-first century, as we teeter on the brink of global catastrophe, it is precisely a shamanistic worldview that is our greatest hope.*

It is my hope that we will move past the desire for titles such as *shaman, master,* and *guru* and truly embrace the challenge of unifying all the beings of our planet and living in harmony and balance with all that surrounds us. There is reason to be optimistic. Movements in areas such as homeopathic and natural medicine, ecopsychology, bioregionalism, deep ecology, green economics, ecofeminism, and ecotherapy among others are paving the way for science, spirit, and people to come together in a healthy and productive way.

With the sharing of these Earthwalks I hope to contribute in some small way to the healing of humanity and our mother, Earth, while at the same time fulfilling a personal vision on the path of life I am walking. I sincerely hope that this book will become a torn and tattered part of your book collection, worn from its journey with you as you make these Earthwalks part of your own personal life path of discovery and magic.

---

*Leslie Gray, "Shamanic Counseling and Ecopsychology," in Theodore Roszak, Mary E. Gomes, and Allen D. Kanner, eds., *Ecopsychology: Restoring the Earth, Healing the Mind* (San Francisco: Sierra Club Books, 1995).

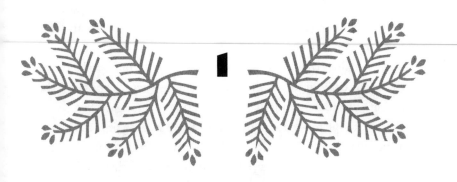

Earthwalks:
What, Why, and How

EARTHWALKS

From the moment my best friend and companion died when I was fourteen years old, I have been a searcher, a seeker looking for the answers to the age-old questions about life and death and why we are here. This best friend of mine who left the world when I was so young happened to be my father. Lucky for me, before his time came he gave me two gifts that would ultimately save my life: freedom and a backyard that was a seemingly endless wilderness of mountains, trees, streams, and meadows. I could walk freely there and explore the world of Nature to my heart's content. My parents were born under communist rule in Hungary but managed to escape to a place of freedom. When it came time to choose a spot where they could live and raise my sister and me, I'm sure that the idea of freedom played an important role in their decision—and I will be eternally grateful, because it was there in those mountains of my childhood that I first came to know the natural world.

Of course, back then I simply took for granted the time I spent outdoors; I was too young to know any better. Running with deer, kicking up pheasants, dodging sunbathing snakes, and listening to raccoons in the night were simply the things I did for fun. I had my special places in the tall pines where I could sit and feel the absolute stillness around me, my secret pond where I watched the animals come to drink and where I caught tadpoles and frogs and snakes. I had my high meadow where I would lie in the tall grass as the wind blew and the sun warmed, and my dark caves where the sun never came but the mystery of the shadows prevailed and dared.

But deep inside of me, beyond the adventure of discovery and exploring every square inch of my wilderness, was the feeling and sense of Nature that can't be explained using words. The harmony and balance of life that is expressed by the songs of the birds in the early-morning sun and the flow of the water as it makes its way to the sea infused my being with little or no awareness on my part. I did not know then that I was walking the same paths and feeling the same magic that had animated so many great people who had come before me, including some I would later come to respect and honor for their eloquent words and deeds—people like Henry David Thoreau, John Muir, Gary Snyder, Victor Sanchez.

As we all know, it takes sorrow to fully appreciate joy, and bondage to truly know freedom. I would have to endure many years of lessons and pain before I could genuinely understand what the forces of Nature were teaching me in my youth. When my father died and I began my quest for answers, I was torn between my feelings of love for life and wilderness and my anger and confusion over my loss. I sought to escape, and escape I did. I ran blindly into anything that would ease my pain, allow me to forget, or provide me with an answer, however short-lived or inaccurate that answer was. I left my home, my school, and my friends and turned my back on all those beings in Nature that had always nurtured my soul. For the next five years I took a trip into the dark side of myself, living on booze, psychedelics, and cheap thrills. I got into fights, crashed cars, dealt drugs, and caused mayhem wherever I went.

And I went to a lot of places. By the time I was eighteen I had been through more than twenty-five states and had lived in stolen cars, mountain shacks, and cheap hotels. The one and only redeeming quality I maintained—the one to which I attribute the saving of my life—was my continued love for the outdoors. Because of this love, even through this dark period of my life, I needed to be in the natural world, and so I ended up spending most of my winters skiing in the Rocky Mountains and the summers swimming and partying by the ocean. In some unexplainable way my awareness of the majesty of those mountains and the endless chant of the ocean tempered my youthful aggressiveness just enough so that my life did not come to an end at the bottom of a glass or in a car wrapped around a telephone pole.

Eventually, though, my lessons arrived in the same way I lived my life, fast and hard. In a period of two short months I was arrested and kicked out of my favorite place in the world, Colorado; I was in a car crash that left me with a broken jaw and my mouth wired shut for six weeks; I broke my left hand in a fistfight; and worst of all, I was looking at possibly spending the next five years or so in jail. The very real possibility of losing my freedom coupled with the inability to speak because of my broken jaw served finally to scare me into waking from the fog of my distorted view of reality.

I went back to school and began to learn a trade I truly loved, photography. But moving back into society and going to school again were not easy tasks, and I was still carrying that burning desire for the answers to my questions. So to help deal with the pressures of trying to shed my addictions, develop a career, and search for my answers, I turned to studying and practicing Eastern religions, Native American teachings, and mysticism. I explored the spiritual use of psychedelics and psychotropic plants. I read everything from the *Bhagavad-Gita* to the *Tao-te ching*, from Castaneda to the Tibetan *Book of the Dead*. I was fully a seeker again, on a spiritual search for my soul and path in life—but this time I had found ancient tools to guide me. They helped me to understand the diversity and richness of spiritual traditions and ancient techniques and philosophies, and helped me to understand more about myself during the process. But I could not believe in any one tradition and I still felt a deep longing to discover who I was and where I fit in.

So it was that after many years dedicated to career, responsibilities, and searching for the spiritual answers to my life, I started to come around full circle to the one entity that truly nurtured my soul—Nature. I took to walking again and immersing myself in the energy of forests, deserts, lakes, and oceans. For the first time in my life I was walking a path that I could truly believe in—one that wound its way between two worlds—the demands of modern society and the mystery and magic of everything I found outdoors. On this path I found a precious balance between the two.

But still there was something missing: companionship. I knew no one else who understood what it meant to try and live in those two worlds at once. I was aware only of people who lived on one side or the other, either secluded in the wilderness or trapped in the city. It was in this period of searching that I first found my connection to the ancient Toltecs of Mexico.

Actually, my first encounter was with Victor Sanchez, a modern-day Toltec. Sanchez was conducting workshops on acquiring knowledge relating to the hidden and magical facets of human awareness through the development of practical techniques based on the writings of Carlos Castaneda and on his experiences with the Mexican Toltec Indians. I went to Mexico to see this work for myself and finally found what I had been searching for: a group of people who used practical techniques to raise the quality of their lives by forming a bridge between the modern world and the magical world of Nature and spirit. And best of all, I didn't have to believe anyone—this work encouraged discovering and experiencing everything for yourself. Even though some activities were done in groups, there were no masters or preachers or gurus. If you didn't do the work, no one told you what you missed or what you were to do next. The lessons were active—many included walking, and the experiences occurred almost exclusively in the world of Nature. This was the start of a magical journey for me. I took the techniques of Sanchez and the Toltec Indians and I started practicing.

During the following years I learned about energy—how to use what I had, how to collect more, how to move it in positive ways, how to connect to and separate from other forms of energy, and so on. I worked for years with Victor's technique of recapitulation—a procedure of self-healing involving reliving events of the past to repair the energetic damage we have incurred—to break free from the limitations and addictions of my past. I took to walking everywhere, fasting for long periods of time in Nature, and I learned to communicate with animals and other powers, including Grandfather Fire. I traveled constantly so that I could walk amid all kinds of natural beauty and majesty and experience the energy and magic of many ancient places of power, including the sites of the ancient Toltecs, Maya, and Aztecs throughout Mexico. I drummed, danced, and sang in all-night ceremonies and stalked my weaknesses to learn what I was truly made of. And eventually, when my energy was in its proper state, I was introduced to the surviving Huichol Indians, who live isolated in the mountains of Mexico, the keepers of the ancient Toltec tradition that embodies the balance between humans and Nature.

Eventually I began to help Victor Sanchez and his organization, the Art of Living Purposefully, to facilitate workshops in Mexico and the United States. Victor himself, who had been presenting workshops for more than twenty years, and his companions Manolo Cetina and Armando Cruz, instructed me over a five-year period in the art of sharing with groups the powerful methodology Sanchez had developed.

As I worked with groups, I began to realize that what I had been doing during my twenty years of searching was simply *learning how to walk*. Victor, Manolo, and Armando once told me that "learning to walk is learning to live." Now I understood what they meant. I had learned how to walk in a way that made me conscientiously observe what I was doing and how these actions affected the world around me. In my walking I had learned to connect myself to the energies and powers of Nature and animals. By putting one foot in front of the other in this way, I had learned who I was and had arrived, years later, at a place of love and joy—that same place I had known as a child but had lost through the complexities of life and living in the modern world.

I could never have made this magical trip by looking out the window of a car or office building, or by reading books or engaging in intellectual conversations. The moments of greatest discovery came when I walked, placing myself physically and energetically into the situations that allowed me to learn, giving myself the opportunity to walk into and out of lessons as I needed them—which is precisely the opportunity I hope to open for you here.

But the techniques presented here are relevant not only for people searching for a spiritual or healing path. It is important for everyone to walk toward the visible face of the spirit of Nature and away from the destructive habits and ways of living that are so much a part of our industrialized society. It doesn't matter what belief system you hold in your heart—these walks are valid for everyone who lives on this marvelous Earth because they stimulate the use of human energy in a way that encourages us to live more healthy, joyous, and connected lives. To walk a path that uses our powerful human potential in a balanced way is one of the noblest pursuits that we can seek in this life on Earth.

❖ The Endless School ❖

Walking is an endless school of mysteries and magic; its instructors, the forces of Nature, the energy of animals and trees. It is the truest form of movement that we have been given, an expression of our lives and a way to experience the sacred places on Earth and the spiritual wonders of the wild. Through walking we can look at our lives and our place in the grand scheme with new eyes while in communion with everything surrounding us.

This book is about walking in ways that require attention, concentration, openness, and courage. The benefits of these walking practices are unlimited and dictated only by how far you wish to take each method. The walks can be used simply as a form of physical exercise and recreation that can be healthy, enjoyable, and fun, or they can be taken to a higher level, becoming something like deep meditation, shamanic trance, and even religious experience. Some of these practices are easily learned, while others can take a lifetime. The same can be said for the results—some are immediate and others require time and patience.

❖ Walking to Better Health ❖

Having been an avid walker, hiker, and climber my whole life, I have seen in my companions and in myself the many health benefits of regular exercise. Even though *Earthwalks for Body and Spirit* aspires to be a book that takes walking far beyond being simply a form of physical exercise, the sedentary lifestyle that is promoted by our world of modern conveniences makes it important for us not to downplay the physical benefits. Walking in particular has gained acceptance by holistic healers as well as the medical community as an activity that promotes health, prevents disease, and extends life span.

As more and more studies are conducted, the benefits of walking can be easily documented. Some of the most recent studies confirm that regular walking can cut the risk of heart attack, stroke, diabetes, heart disease, breast cancer, and arterial disease. Regular walking can also help prevent osteoporosis and can reduce body fat. The increase in blood flow created by rapid walking also causes the frontal areas of the brain to take in additional oxygen, a process that increases the brain's reaction time and heightens our ability to ignore distractions and complete mental tasks. The list of health benefits from many reliable sources of information goes on and on.

❖ Walking in Nature ❖

For me, walking is much more than simply a healthy way to exercise the physical body, especially walking in Nature, which provides a chance to leave behind the concerns of our daily lives, if only briefly, and to feast our senses on colors, sounds, and scents that can add beauty and wonder to our lives. As Henry David Thoreau wrote more than one hundred years ago:

[T]he walking of which I speak has nothing in it akin to taking exercise, as it is called, as the sick take medicine at stated hours— as the swinging of dumb-bells or chairs; but is itself the enterprise of the day . . . When we walk we naturally go to the fields and woods; what would become of us if we walked only in a garden or mall?*

A sad circumstance of our industrial world is that for many people Nature is something that is seen only in magazines, on the Discovery Channel, or in photographs by Ansel Adams. My friends, this has to change. Unless we all learn the importance of our connection to the natural world we will continue down the path of destruction that promises to end in planetary genocide. Our connection lives in our preserved tracts of wilderness, our backyards, our parks, and even in that one lone tree that stands by the side of the highway.

It is no great mystery how we become disconnected from Earth. It begins in childhood when we are separated from her and educated in indoor classrooms filled with media and books. Dr. Michael J. Cohen, an educator with over thirty-five years of experience teaching the merits of reconnecting with Nature, puts it this way:

The authorities in our modern lives—parents, educators, presidents—teach us to spend an average of over 95 percent of our life indoors. For example, we are "sentenced" to spending over 18,000 hours of our developmental childhood years indoors in classrooms or else suffer the pains of truancy . . . Learning to tolerate excessive existence indoors is as much a part of our education as are books, videos, and lectures. We educate ourselves with indoor thinking, media, and responsibilities to the extent that we average less than one day per lifetime in sensory tune with the natural world.†

---

*Henry David Thoreau, *Walking* (Boston: Beacon Press, 1991).

†Michael J. Cohen, Ed.D., *Reconnecting with Nature: Finding Wellness through Restoring Your Bond with the Earth* (Corvallis, Ore.: Ecopress, 1997).

But we are not destined to remain on this path. We are children of Earth—of Sun, Water, Wind, and Fire. We human beings are the caretakers of Earth, not the spoiled little children who bite the hand that feeds them. We have a sacred responsibility to protect and care for our mother. I invite and implore you to begin walking with Nature as a regular activity that will help you understand and fulfill your sacred obligation to her.

❖ Connecting or Conquering? ❖

An interesting, and to my mind sad, trend in recent years is the manner in which people in industrialized countries have begun to "get back to Nature." Outdoor activities such as mountain biking, snowboarding, kayaking, and mountaineering, to name a few, are now extremely popular, as are outdoor courses and wilderness empowerment workshops designed for the corporate world. The sad thing to me is not that people are spending time outdoors, but that they are doing so without an awareness of what they are doing and why. All too often activities are centered on the challenge of conquering Nature rather than becoming one with it. It seems to me that an important part of spending time outdoors is to periodically stop and ask ourselves what it is we are doing there and why: Am I involved in an activity that simply demonstrates another manifestation of anthropocentrism? Am I involved in this activity in Nature so as to conquer it for enjoyment or personal empowerment, or am I really connecting to it in a meaningful way? In asking ourselves these questions, we begin to see through the eyes of Nature—good medicine for people in industrialized regions of the world.

❖ What Are Earthwalks? ❖

What I wish to share with you in the following Earthwalks are some techniques to help you realize a significant and positive energetic change that can dramatically improve your life. These walks have the ability to move energy in very precise ways that lead to personal transformation and healing for both yourself and Earth by allowing you to see your life and actions from the perspective of the natural world. They are walking practices that blend the physical aspects of exercise with exposure to the inexhaustible mysteries and energy of the world of Nature. These techniques of walking produce states of awareness that focus attention, heal wounds, and develop reciprocity with all that surrounds us. They celebrate our desire to balance our relationship with Earth with the magic and mystery that live inside us.

These walks invite you to leave behind the controlling sides of your rational mind and ego in order to discover something new. To facilitate this process, each Earthwalk has a unique theme that is used to catch your attention and activities to perform as you travel that will help you to enter into the heart and spirit of the walk. Some of the Earthwalks open doors to new and exciting experiences by moving your attention away from the concerns of your daily life and then adding elements that promote healthy interaction with the natural world. Others are used to bring your personal real-world struggles to the forefront as you walk, then connect your energy with specific forces of Nature to heighten your natural insight and allow healing of your problems and challenges.

Many sources of knowledge have contributed to the creation of these Earthwalks. My first introduction to walking practices that actually had structural components was through Victor Sanchez's Art of Living Purposefully workshops in Mexico. Many of the walks in this book have come directly from or were inspired by my participation in or instruction of these workshops. From my connection and friendship with Victor and his companions I was also introduced to the world of the Huichol Indians, who live in the isolated mountains of western Mexico. Their lives of connection to Earth and spirit have inspired my views of the relationship between human beings and the forces of Nature to ascend to a new level. Many of the Earthwalks come from this inspiration and the Huichol Indians' profound influence on my life.

❖ How to Use This Book ❖

Each of the Earthwalks presented here has its own unique energy and feeling. While the book has been divided into several parts for ease of reference and practice, there are certainly overlapping themes in the walks themselves. Each of the walks can be used in a variety of ways. You might simply choose one, review the steps, and begin. Or you could read some of the descriptions of the walks and add these elements to your own daily walking regimen. There are really no rules for use of what's shared here. However, the order in which the walks are presented here *is* meaningful, and to experience the most from them, I recommend that you start with the first walk and then proceed numerically. Each walk will stimulate the use of your attention and energy in a way that will prepare you for the next one. It is entirely possible to gain beneficial effects from the walks by skipping around the book, but these benefits will be more profound as you progress through the practices consecutively and as you develop the rhythm that is implied by the order in which they are presented. I traveled for years practicing the very first Earthwalk of this book—Walk 1, Walk of Attention—and from that practice I was better able to enter into other walks that required different and sometimes even higher levels of attention, such as Walk 8, Walk of Silence, or Walk 14, Into the Unknown.

The presentation of each of the walks follows the same structure: introductory information, followed by a set of numbered descriptive instructions on how to perform the walk (these will be less specific for those walks that are to be somewhat self-designed based, in some instances, on your personal situation and energy), and concluding most often with comments that relate to each particular walking practice.

I suggest that before beginning each walk you first read its entire description to familiarize yourself with the theme of the walk, the specific steps, and the comments about its practice—and remember that you may not fully grasp the whys and hows of a specific walk until you actually experience it. Because each walk involves learning the mysteries of the natural world, it will be difficult to understand the heart of any of them by simply reading their descriptions; when you bring them into the world of action you will be able to fully realize their purpose and effect.

The very nature of the practices of walking in this book allows them to be used in a variety of ways. As already stated, the recommended way to realize the full potential and lessons in the walks is to do them in order. But certainly there will be the temptation to first practice those that you feel attracted to. While this is fine, remember that the part of yourself that chooses what it likes best is precisely the part of yourself that these walks are trying to slow down—the dominant, "in control" part that may look for an immediate result. Nature is the perfect arena in which to tame this impulse, allow you to discover your hidden potential, and heighten your awareness. The point here is to try something new. Give yourself the chance to experience the feeling of doing something completely foreign to you or something that you think isn't necessary. This is an important path of growth and learning, and walking it will open doors for you that you never even knew were there.

These walks can be done alone, with friends, or even with large groups. The more you experience them, the more you will realize how flexible they are. You can integrate them into walks that are already a part of your day or into your ongoing spiritual life. If you perform a walk but don't seem to "get it," simply try it again some other time. Remember that some of the indigenous people who originated a good many of these techniques spent a lifetime working toward fully experiencing them. What's more, the lessons of Earthwalks reveal themselves at various depths and levels as you yourself grow. There are no rules here. Proceed as your own heart dictates, and your experiences and lessons will unfold under the watchful eye of Mother Earth and the powers and forces that guide her.

❖ Key Words ❖

Translating into words our remarkable and humbling experiences in the world of Nature can be a supreme challenge, and trying to describe to another person how to experience something similar is even more difficult. Adding to the difficulty is the fact that each of us has a unique personal history, cultural bias, and education, and therefore a unique personal interpretation of what specific words mean. For this reason it seems appropriate to include here a brief alphabetical summary of some key words in this book and how they are used. As you get to know how I use these words, you may even change some of them to words that are more resonant for you. Take, for example, the word *energy*. Depending on the context, some people might prefer to substitute the term *life force* or *essence*—both of which are fine. Use whatever words hold the most significance for you. But in the end, my suggestion is not to get hung up on the words—use the words and descriptions to jump into the experience, and from there the need for words becomes much less important.

- *Attention.* This is the magical gift that allows us to use our consciousness. Attention can be trained to focus, expand, and unite. The power of attention allows us to concentrate on a single act to such a degree that the rest of the world disappears and we become one with the action. This ability, however, can also trap us in a single-minded view of the world that blinds us to the reality of the existence of other ways of living and being. The magic of attention can take us to beautiful places that we can scarcely imagine, or can trap us in a living nightmare. Earthwalks focus our attention on activities that are different from those we are normally accustomed to, and cause a rift in the continuity of our perception. Through this opening a new view can emerge and grow. With continued attention to these "foreign" activities it is possible to enter into levels of inner silence, connection to outside energy, and heightened perception and awareness. Using our energy on this kind of attention is one of the most exciting and interesting experiences that we can have as human beings. The walks presented here are not only an invitation to explore new levels of attention; they are a practical means to accomplish this. They can deliver you to amazing worlds of experience that go far beyond simply watching, thinking, reading, or imagining.

- *AVP.* This is the acronym for El Arte de Vivir a Proposito, the Art of Living Purposefully, which is a group founded by anthropologist and author Victor Sanchez more than twenty years ago to maintain a deep connection to the knowledge of the Toltecs and to carry this knowledge to others through, in part, modifying Toltec practices and perspectives so that people in our modern society may benefit from them. AVP conducts workshops worldwide that are centered on sharing the hidden treasures of indigenous knowledge.

- *Connection.* Our desire to connect with the things around us prompts us to enter into the realm of pure action in order to reclaim our lost unity to all the beings on this wonderful planet. This can truly expand our perception of the world in a profound way. True connection results in a relationship of give and take, which leads to the most personal experience of the mystery of the world of Nature.

- *Energy.* Everything in the universe, including human beings, is composed of energy, and everything is connected at the level of energy. Earthwalks invite you to view the people, situations, and things of your daily life on an energetic level, which usually results in an improved perspective. By viewing another person as a luminous field of energy, and not simply as another personality controlled by a brain or ego, it becomes easier to communicate clearly, without manipulation or misunderstanding. Our energetic connection with all that surrounds us results in actions of consideration and good faith—if we are energetically connected to everything around us, then we cannot want to hurt another person or an element of the natural world. Walking in a manner that puts you in touch with how you interact with the world on an energetic level is a grand start to living an energetically healthy life by opening the door to experiencing the synchronicity and magic of all that's living and the magic of a life in which dreams become reality.

- *Huichol.* The Huichol Indians (who refer to themselves as the Wirrarika) live in remote areas of the Sierra Madres in western Mexico. Although some of their villages located close to Mexican towns have been influenced by contemporary civilization, there still exist the core villages that remain almost entirely separate from the modern world. These communities have no roads, electricity, or other modern influences and their people preserve the ancient tradition of living within the sacred reality of Earth. Their simple but happy lives and their deep Nature-based spirituality continue to be a great source of inspiration for those who wish to challenge themselves to evolve into kinder, more deeply feeling human beings.

- *Inner silence.* In almost every tradition promoting the quest for self-knowledge there exist practices for quieting the mind. Although the specific motivations and techniques may differ from one tradition to another, the underlying message is that achieving a state of inner silence has numerous benefits for human beings. Many traditions, especially in the East, value the elimination of desire as a key to inner silence. By reducing the importance placed upon materialistic goals, romantic desires, social obligations, and so forth, the practitioner places himself in a position to quiet the incessant chatter in the mind related to these activities. There are also traditions in which a specific vehicle is used to introduce a "block" to the internal dialogue. Drumming, chanting, ritual dancing, forms of meditation, fasting, prayer, and walking with attention, for example, are each used in a wide variety of ways to help practitioners reach those moments when the internal chatter loses its power and the door opens to allow an experience of the world from a point of view decidedly different from the single-minded "I" perspective. This is the moment when the world of our usual perception opens out to the worlds that we have lost by erecting reason as our king.

- *Intention.* Your intention is the force you employ to explore the themes of individual Earthwalks. Just as a baseball player intends to hit the ball with his bat, you intend to accomplish the specific theme of each walk. As an instructional step, many of these walks ask that you state out loud your intention before you begin walking so that you are clear with yourself and Earth, which enables you to guide your attention.

    During the energetic exchange that takes place during and after an offering—especially one that relates to the future—your intention will guide your actions toward the fulfillment of your commitment.

- *Perception.* The expansion of what we are able to perceive in the natural world by using our senses and all the other resources that we have as human beings is a central goal of the walks shared here. As these forms of walking are introduced into your life and practiced over a period of time, they will begin to challenge your boundaries of perception. Earthwalks provide the opportunity to see through the eyes of Nature that our perceptions derive from our current interpretation of our reality, and that there are techniques that can be employed to help us perceive our reality from different and often improved perspectives.

- *Self-observation.* This phrase refers to viewing yourself and your actions without interference from the controlling side of your ego. Its hallmark is the objectivity you might have if you could see yourself with a different set of eyes. Earthwalks invite you to observe yourself specifically through the eyes of Nature.

- *Toltec.* I use this word in the context of how it was taught to me rather than in the way that most anthropologists or archaeologists use it. My understanding of the word is the same as that of the ancient Aztecs, roughly translating to "person of knowledge." The Toltecs I speak of fall more or less into three categories: the ancient Toltecs, the surviving Toltecs, and the new Toltecs.

  The ancient Toltecs were actually much different from how they were depicted by the Europeans who conquered them or the anthropologists who have since studied them from a limited cultural perspective. These ancient Toltecs were highly developed culturally, technologically, and spiritually and extended their influence to many other cultures throughout the Americas. They embodied the practice of integrating the spiritual and rational parts of humanity to live in harmony with self and the world of Nature—a practice that our modern, industrialized, Newtonian culture has tragically lost.

  The surviving Toltecs are the indigenous people who keep alive the tradition of the ancient Toltecs even today, such as the Huichol people of the mountains of western Mexico.

  The new Toltecs are those people, either indigenous or nonindigenous, who follow the path of the ancient Toltecs. They seek to create a balance between the modern world and the world of Nature and spirit through specific techniques that can be shared and lived by all people.

❖ Learning How to Walk ❖

For most people walking is an activity that requires no thought or intention—because we have done it almost our whole lives, it is rarely even a conscious action. What's more, since walking is such a natural act, we are able to involve ourselves in a host of other activities while doing it. Because we most often walk to get from one place to the next, it is quite common for us to talk, eat, think, or even read while walking. Because of this, we seldom pay any attention to how we walk or to how the people around us walk. But watching other people walk is one of the best ways to discover who they are and can also provide you with clues to how you yourself walk.

This observation of other people starts as an exercise but can evolve into an important tool. Understanding how walking reflects the inner being of the walker is a valuable skill for interacting in the world. To begin your observation, place yourself in a position where you can observe lots of people walking. Notice the variety of physical walking styles and pay attention to any patterns that arise. Does someone with an angry scowl usually walk fast or slow? How is a child's walk different from an adult's? Do females walk differently from males? How do body position and balance affect a person's walk—is a person's head leaning forward or is it straight, is the body leaning into the direction of motion or away from it, is the stride short and rapid or long and slow?

Although people walk in a variety of ways, there are some universal aspects to most people's walking that stem from our lives in the modern world and reflect the inner attitudes that are so often produced by an industrialized culture. In this book you will learn how to undo many of these "habits." For instance, many people experience wandering attention when they walk, a result of time spent in a world that requires us to think about many things at the same time—so in these Earthwalks you will concentrate on focusing attention in very specific ways. Most people walk with their bodies moving willy-nilly, their centers of gravity and balance shifting uncontrollably. In these walks you will learn to move with fluidity and equilibrium.

An interesting point to note before you begin is that Earthwalks do not require any experience with walking in Nature. On the contrary, I have witnessed countless times that experienced hikers are sometimes the most jaded, and that people with less experience in the natural world are far more open to receiving its lessons. Perhaps this is because hiking is so goal-oriented, involving traveling to a destination—often over rough terrain—and then returning. Sometimes the accomplishment of the goal overrides everything else, including stopping to smell the roses or enjoying more than superficially the unique energy of the area through which you are moving. The walks in this book, each with its own theme and intention, remind us that there is an unlimited number of ways to walk through the world.

Walking with intention is a valuable technique to enjoy and use throughout life, reflecting a proactive state of being and attitude toward the future. It can help build strength and confidence to meet the world in a way that is as fluid as the water in a flowing river rather than as stop-and-start as a car stuck in a traffic jam. This state of being can be applied to all aspects of life and can spread from you to all those around you.

❖ Creating a Sacred Space ❖

Performing Earthwalks will naturally lead to periods of time in which you take yourself out of your normal environment and state of being. While these times can be special and magical respites from the demands of modern life, they should be viewed as more than merely mini-vacations or rest breaks. These walks are best performed when you begin them with the intention of learning something about yourself and the world around you. Performing them can be viewed as walking the path of knowledge or as walking sacred ground, suggesting the importance of your practice.

It will be beneficial to arrive at the starting place of your walk in a state of being that is intentional and planned. Except for the Earthwalks that directly confront elements of your daily life, you should begin each walk in a state that will allow you to perform with a minimum of distracting thoughts about your day. In most cases it is best to make a conscious effort to take care of whatever you need to do before going for your walk—getting the affairs of your day in order, making sure you have time allocated for the exercise so that you are not worrying about eating, going to the bathroom, getting something into the mail, and so on.

Creating this kind of time for yourself has many advantages in terms of performing the walks and raising your quality of life. Walking outdoors, reflecting, and exercising are activities that are commonly robbed from us by today's fast-paced, time-starved world.

❖ Walking Safely ❖

You *must* remain responsible for your own safety at all times while walking. If you are walking in an unfamiliar area, make sure ahead of time that it is a safe place to travel in solitude and understand that you will need to be even more aware of your surroundings in order not to get lost, fall on uneven ground, or travel into territory where people might be hunting, for example. The main rule is simply to use common sense. Dress appropriately for the season, wear comfortable shoes, and don't walk near dangerous areas such as quarries and landfills or in areas that are known as magnets for illegal activity. Be especially aware if you are traveling alone in an area removed from other people or if darkness is approaching— especially if you are a woman. It's a sad fact in our modern society that women in particular are not always safe from harm in Nature's quiet and removed places.

If you are new to walking long distances, keep your walks short until you build endurance. If you take medication for any type of serious illness, don't go walking without it. Listen to your body—it can communicate both positive and negative conditions, and re-member that not all of these are caused by the obvious. Weariness may not be related to the way you walk or the distance you walk so much as to your diet or the way you deal with stress. Though I have easily climbed tall mountains during a long fast, I have also taken walks during which I felt tired after only a few steps because I was carrying a big load of sadness or self-pity on my back. The point is that many things contribute to physical performance; it's important to build awareness of the relationship you have with your body and practice common sense while you perform your Earthwalks.

2

Walks of Attention

ATTENTION

From the first moment I was introduced to the art of walking with attention, my view of walking was altered forever—and so was my life. These walking practices opened a door to completely new states of awareness for me, resulting in profound insights regarding how I perceived the world, Nature, and my own internal process.

The key to unlocking this door is learning specific techniques that focus the attention on those things that we don't usually see or feel. The Earthwalks in this section remove the veil that has been placed over our senses, allowing us to truly notice the world and encounter that part of ourselves that is yearning to be out in the open. These practices can allow you to approach Nature on an extremely practical level—which first leads to the restoration of a more Nature-centered perception and thus the restoration of our sacred bond with Earth. It then leads to our awareness of Mother Earth's incalculable love, support, and knowledge, which help us manage the stress and strain of our modern lifestyles.

You will begin with developing attention and balance in your walking so that all of the subsequent walks in this book can be performed in a manner that is best suited to the natural world. Next, you will move into practices of walking that focus on increased awareness of the magic in our natural surroundings. This practice may include performing walks that are foreign to you, and will lead to perceptions that are unusual for you. Ultimately, all that you have gained from increasing your attention through these practices, all the insights you have gleaned from learning to look at the natural world in a new way, will help you to look inside yourself with new eyes. It is this process that helps you to arrive at a separate reality of the possibilities you possess.

The Fox Stance

The Fox Stance is named in honor of our brother the fox, a highly alert being whose movements embody awareness and connection to his surroundings. He and the deer that live in mountainous regions are my two favorite teachers of walking—but learning from them involves far more than merely mimicking their movements. Each step of the fox is deliberate, taken with full attention and energy. All his senses are receiving information from his surroundings and all their beings. His motions and actions are fluid and do not disturb the environment. The walk of the fox is like a dance of expression.

The Fox Stance is not actually a walk; it is a position of the body adopted directly before you begin to walk in order to establish a base from which all walks can grow and blossom. Many of the following Earthwalks start from this stance.

Instructions for the Practice

1. To begin, stand with your feet shoulder-width apart.

2. Take a step forward with your left foot but leave the right foot where it is.

3. Position your upper body slightly forward but with more of your weight on your back foot. This will not be easy at first. By putting more of your weight on your back foot, your back knee will probably be bent slightly more than the front.

4. Arms are held in a comfortable position at your sides.

5. Adopt an unfamiliar position with your hands. For more specific information, see Comments on the Practice, below.

6. Take a few deep breaths and state out loud the intention of your walk.

Comments on the Practice

This is the basic starting position for most walks—by adopting it you have already created a way for your walk to begin that is unique and not part of your everyday world. This stance prepares you for your journey.

By placing more weight on your back foot than on your front, you will negate your automatic commitment to the next step. Normally we walk by swinging our legs and dropping our weight firmly on the heel of the front foot, but this is a blundering style in the outdoors. It is noisy, damaging to the foliage and insects underfoot and around us, clumsy, and inefficient. When walking in an attentive manner it is far better to place the front foot where you want it to go. In this way you can increase control if you need to stop suddenly, you can walk much more quietly, and you can more easily avoid stepping on a beautiful insect, a lovely plant, or a rusty piece of metal hidden in the grass.

Pay special attention to adopting a position with your hands. First of all, it will necessitate that you carry nothing. If you need to take things with you on your walk, use pockets, a fanny pack, or a backpack. Second, adopting a position with the hands will cause you to focus attention on them. You can hold your hands in any position that feels comfortable: a loose fist, two fingers out and the rest curled, or all curled in a loose fist except the thumb, for example.

Stating the intention of the walk is a simple and concrete way of gathering your attention and announcing your intention to your surroundings. In the beginning it is common to feel awkward doing this, but do it anyway. And simply saying it silently, in your mind, is not enough—it is far more powerful to state your intention out loud, in a clear voice. A lengthy speech is not necessary; a few words will do just fine. As human beings, we have developed to a high level our ability to use our voice as a means of expression, and in terms of energy it is a powerful tool.

1. Walk of Attention

By adding certain special elements, we can convert a simple walk into a walk of attention. Although everyone apparently "knows how" to walk, the fact of the matter is—for modern people—to walk correctly requires special training that also tends to yield special results.

VICTOR SANCHEZ*

The Walk of Attention is the practice upon which all Earthwalks are based—its key elements will become the core of your future practice. This was the very first structured form of walking I learned and it comes from my friend and companion Victor Sanchez. By practicing it you will transform the act of walking from something mundane into a form of movement that expresses your dreams and inner desire for knowledge and balance. Ultimately, it provides a way to walk through life.

Instructions for the Practice

1. Start in the Fox Stance, making sure to adopt a position with your hands. For further explanation of this, see Comments on the Practice in the Fox Stance, page 26.

2. Begin walking in silence, moving with a rhythm that feels natural to you. Remember that the speed is not important.

3. As you walk, focus attention on your breathing, working toward matching it to the rhythm of your walk.

4. Begin to focus your attention on the sounds, scents, and other elements of your surroundings, taking care not to allow your thoughts to distract you. Try to neither stop them nor give them

---

*Victor Sanchez, *The Teachings of Don Carlos: Practical Applications of the Works of Carlos Castaneda* (Santa Fe: Bear & Company, 1995).

special attention, but instead simply listen to them as though they are part of the sounds around you.

5. Be alert to how your body feels while you are walking.

Comments on the Practice

Walking in silence opens the door to experiences that are separate from the familiar, language-based events and situations that dominate our lives. Experiences that do not include talking, reading, listening, or responding to words allow us to encounter knowledge and insight in a completely different way by inviting us to understand the powerful communication of Nature that we can explore in full only when we learn to listen with our whole body and all of our senses.

Creating a rhythm for your walk and developing the ability to match your breathing to it will come naturally as you practice. The same applies to hearing your thoughts as one more set of sounds among all the others around you. This is a challenge that can be met by consciously allowing the walk and your thoughts to flow together in a harmonious way—be patient; it may take time.

While walking in this way, notice how your body feels and be alert to what it is telling you. To do this, first relax into the walk, which will loosen the rigidity of your ego and allow deep body sensations to become more accessible to you. Next, instead of simply thinking about a certain part of your body, let your attention flow gently into it. Start by focusing your awareness on your shoulders, then your stomach, and then your legs. Focus too on your heart, genital area, spine, scalp, lungs, feet, buttocks. Explore how these areas feel by allowing your body to tell you which ones feel alive, strong, and vital, and which feel heavy, tight, dull, or in pain. This information can give you further insight into your diet, level of physical activity, daily habits, and lifestyle. Remember that the microcosm of your body can in many ways be seen as an expression of the macrocosm of your life. While our ego spends much of its time looking toward the future or lamenting over the past, our body lives in and reflects the concrete present.

Because we are a blend of body, mind, and spirit, raising the awareness of our total human organism can make us more sensitive to the living systems of Earth and to the sacred unity between our body and the Earth body.

2. Walk of Balance

Walking is the great adventure, the first meditation, a practice of heartiness and soul primary to humankind. Walking is the exact balance between spirit and humility.

GARY SNYDER*

The twofold intention behind this walk is to learn to move in a way that is friendly to the natural world and to develop within our bodies a balanced gait. The usual way we walk resembles a "swing and drop" action resulting in the heel extended out in front of us to come crashing to the ground with the force of our total body weight. This is not only unhealthy for the body but also destructive to the natural world.

Walking with balance and grace reflects not just your physical prowess but your internal state as well. To walk with balance is to successfully meld the opposing forces of left and right, rational and spiritual, ego and energy in a way that echoes the duality of life: The right needs the left to walk upright and straight; our rational mind needs our spiritual insight to maintain balance and health. Life itself is delicately balanced, and making yourself aware of the level of balance you attain as you walk can awaken you to the level of balance in your life as a whole. This walk begins simply; as you proceed through the practices in this book, you can

*Gary Snyder, *The Practice of the Wild* (New York: North Point Press, 1990).

continue to come back to this one, challenging yourself to reach a new level each time. This walk can be performed anywhere outdoors where there is space enough, but the best place would be somewhere with flat terrain suitable for easy and relaxed movement.

Instructions for the Practice

1. Start walking in a relaxed fashion that feels "normal" to you and explore how your body feels as you move.

2. After a few minutes of this movement, consciously shift the focus of your attention on walking with balance and equilibrium by gently and easily "placing" each of your feet on the ground so that your weight isn't committed to your front foot until you want it to be.

3. Continue walking in a way that makes you conscious of each step as you place your feet. You are not tiptoeing, but neither are you walking with your legs swinging and your heels crashing to the ground. Simply walk in a way that feels smooth to you. Refer back to Comments on the Practice in the Fox Stance, page 26, if needed.

4. Walk in this manner for a few minutes and then, at some point, note where your center of balance is and stop in mid-stride. Immediately after stopping, notice again where your center of balance is located. The idea is to walk in such a way that you can keep your foot off the ground, no matter where you stop in your stride, without falling forward, backward, or to the side. Continue walking and stopping at random intervals to see how balanced you are overall. If a partner is working with you, ask that he or she say "stop" at random times—the element of surprise and the unexpected in having someone else direct your movements in this way will allow you to see and feel more effectively how balanced you are.

5. After this initial phase you can move into situations that overtly require balanced walking: Place yourself on a curb, board, log, or anything else that forces you to maintain balance. (Start by walking on something fairly close to the ground so that if you fall off you won't be injured.) As your balance improves, challenge yourself. You can use your partner's help here as well, stopping and starting based on his or her call.

6. Expand your walks to include such surfaces as rocks, fallen trees, the edges of trails or sidewalks, small and rocky streams, and small and steep embankments.

Comments on the Practice

Challenging yourself to stop mid-step is the best way to assess your balance because it allows you to discern immediately and exactly where and how your weight and momentum are traveling. If you stop suddenly and your body continues to move forward, you should adjust your position so that more of your weight is distributed backward. If you stop abruptly mid-step and your raised foot comes down behind you to support your weight, your weight is shifted too far to the back and must be adjusted forward.

Every time you perform this walk, be sure to notice not only your physical balance but your thoughts and feelings as well: How do you feel while walking? How are your thoughts affecting your walk? What are you thinking about? How do you feel when you fall or stumble—are you angry, disappointed, or annoyed? Why? Remember that learning to walk is learning to live. This is a path of attention that will affect your entire life—with the right attitude, it can place you in the realm of fulfillment and magic.

3. Walk of Equilibrium

Left foot / right foot, the walker moves through the landscape.
Right brain / left brain, sensation and reflection flicker into
the complex wholeness of human response.

John Elder*

This is another walk that requires balance, and should be performed after you have thoroughly explored Walk 2, Walk of Balance. Since the Walk of Equilibrium is almost impossible to perform while moving in an inattentive manner, it will compel you to explore a balanced and focused walking style. Perform this walk for a specific duration, whenever and wherever you wish—around the house or deep in the wilderness.

Instructions for the Practice

1. Place a book or other object on the top of your head and begin walking.

2. Explore shifting your weight, modifying your foot placement, and so forth to see how best to keep the object from falling off your head. More than likely you will discover that you need to place your front foot instead of swinging and dropping it. Controlling the shift of your weight—and thus the balance of the object—will require that your weight fall slightly toward your back foot and that your knees bend slightly. All together, this will create for your body a side-to-side and up-and-down state of equilibrium.

3. Try placing other objects on your head—but remember that large, inflexible objects are harder to balance than small, soft ones.

---

*John Elder, introduction to *Walking,* by Henry David Thoreau (Boston: Beacon Press, 1991).

Comments on the Practice

Challenge yourself by trying to balance increasingly difficult items as you walk. The lessons you learn from this practice and the more you perform it will affect the way you walk in wild areas and the physical impact you have on them.

4. Barefoot Walk

It was good for the skin to touch Earth and the old people liked to remove their moccasins and walk with bare feet on the sacred Earth. . . . The soil was soothing, strengthening, cleansing, and healing.

CHIEF LUTHER STANDING BEAR*

Taking off your shoes instantly changes your view of the world. Your personality transforms, you relax and let down your guard, and suddenly you feel that you are not so insulated from the world. The soles of our feet are wonderful sensory organs that we tend to keep wrapped and hidden away—but when they are free to experience the air and earth, the sun and water, they can provide us with a great deal of information that can lead to discovery. Earth, moss, grass, leaves, water, rock, and wood underfoot—a bare foot— provide a whole new world of physical sensation and feeling and, perhaps even more significant, a unique state of mind. Walking barefoot outdoors is a profound means of shedding the everyday, modern world to grow close to Mother Earth and more like the rest of her children—only humans insulate themselves from Earth by covering their feet. This Earthwalk is an invitation for you to let your feet escape their bondage and run free.

Because most of us are not accustomed to walking outdoors without shoes, recognize, before beginning, the importance of common sense and of expanding your perception of the world to include

---

*Chief Luther Standing Bear, quoted by T. C. McLuhan, *Touch the Earth* (New York: Outerbridge & Dienstfrey, 1971).

the fact that shoes aren't absolutely necessary for survival. Note too, however, that the soles of your feet are highly sensitive and will need to be cared for with love and gentleness until they are comfortable with the world again. Part of this care involves thinking of your bare feet as you would a small child who has just learned to walk. You wouldn't take such a child for a five-mile hike in the desert, or let him climb on high rocks. Nor should you do these things barefoot until you are ready. Begin like a child learning to walk—walk in the soft grass, walk around your house, go to a park or nature center where the trails are manicured. Gradually explore all kinds of walking surfaces while being extremely gentle and careful. And above all—enjoy!

Instructions for the Practice

1. Once you've arrived at the place where your walk will begin, remove your shoes and socks and adopt the Fox Stance.

2. Begin walking very slowly in the way you have learned from Walks 2 and 3, Walk of Balance and Walk of Equilibrium. Move attentively, placing your feet exactly where you want them to be as you walk—avoid shuffling or dragging them—and pay extremely close attention to what is on the ground in front of you as you step.

3. If you see something interesting on either side of you, stop to look at it rather than continue walking and looking to the side as you pass it—looking at it as you walk means that you are not watching where you are placing your feet!

4. Breathe deeply and relax while remaining attentive. Walk slowly and feel each new sensation, remembering that it is not uncommon for the first few minutes of barefoot walking in Nature to be an experience of sensory overload. Your feelings may include a sudden and intense love for your surroundings and regret for not having done this sooner—but what matters is

that you're doing it now! If you need to laugh or jump up and down or even cry, then do so! Remember, there are no rules—especially when you walk without shoes!

5. As you get used to the feeling of walking barefoot, challenge yourself to explore many different types of terrain and a variety of surfaces. Puddles; pine needles; soft, cool earth; dry, rocky earth; leaves; stone; wood—each of these has a unique energy and produces a unique sensation, both of which illustrate how diverse Nature is. Open yourself, walk Earth with your bare soles, and you will never be the same again.

Comments on the Practice

Your first few barefoot walks outdoors should be short in duration. By taking short walks two or three times a week, you will probably feel comfortable walking two to three miles after a month or so. It is always a good idea to carry shoes in a knapsack just in case your feet get sore. It is also a good practice to carry plastic bandages and antibacterial ointment.

Barefoot walking is a great activity to pursue with friends, but I have also enjoyed my experiences walking barefoot alone in the middle of the wilderness at a dead-slow speed, each foot soaking up every feeling and sensation with every step. Barefoot walking is like coming home to your true mother.

5. A Child's Eyes

To speak truthfully, few adult persons can see Nature. Most persons do not see the Sun. At least they have a superficial seeing. The Sun illuminates only the eye of the adult, but shines into the eye and the heart of the child. The lover of Nature is the one whose inward and outward senses are still truly adjusted to each other; who has retained the spirit of infancy even into the era of adulthood. Such a person's intercourse with heaven and Earth becomes part of her daily food. In the presence of Nature a wild delight runs through the person, in spite of real sorrows. Nature says—this is my creature, with all his impertinent gifts, he shall be glad with me.

RALPH WALDO EMERSON*

This Earthwalk presents you with the opportunity to transport yourself back in time to your childhood, an age of innocence, wonder, discovery, and joy when the world was one big mystery just waiting to be explored. This time, however, you are the one who sets the rules—and decides there aren't any!

During this walk you are allowed to get dirty, "spill the milk," and "pull the cat's tail" (just kidding)—you are allowed to be very young again. To truly experience the world's magic and wonder, it's imperative that we let go of our belief that we know all things in the world simply because we have names for them or a scientific understanding of them. We adults too often reduce everything to explanations and rational thought and in this sad condition we almost never let ourselves explore the pure mystery that surrounds us every day of our lives. We walk around seeing the same things in the same way until we don't even really see them anymore.

Fortunately, this is a spell that can be broken with sufficient effort, and that is what this walk attempts to accomplish—encouraging you to give yourself the eyes and freedom of a young child whose rules are often as simple as "Do not hurt yourself or others."

Instructions for the Practice

1. Choose an outdoor place and begin Walk 1, Walk of Attention. After about fifteen minutes, change your focus so that as you walk you feel yourself traveling back in time, becoming younger and younger, as young as three or four years old. Don't just imagine it—try to truly feel it. At such an age you are able to walk,

---

*Ralph Waldo Emerson, quoted in Anne Rowthorn, *Earth and All the Stars* (Novato, Calif.: New World Library, 2000).

yet the ideas and views of parents, teachers, and other adults or advertising and media influences have not yet made a significant impression on who you are.

2. Now see and feel with the eyes and body of a child. Walk slowly and start to look at everything around you as though you've never seen it before. Pick things up, smell them, feel them. Chase butterflies, jump into puddles, roll in dirt and mud, examine blades of grass and leaves and flowers, look up at the sky and watch the clouds go by, see the birds for the amazing beings they are, see the magic all around you, fall down, jump into the air—become a child in a world of brand-new discoveries.

Comments on the Practice

Give yourself the chance to really explore this state of being as you walk through nature—and if you have someone to share your walk with you, all the better. When you have finished, try not to be finished. Keep this feeling with you; allow yourself to explore in this same way all things on your life's path and you will discover that magic is everywhere.

6. Count Three

Step out onto the Planet. Draw a circle a hundred feet round.
Inside the circle are 300 things nobody understands, and,
maybe nobody's ever seen. How many can you find?

LEW WELCH*

Armando Cruz, a longtime instructor of the Art of Living Purposefully and my good friend, has spent many years developing techniques of body movement designed to increase attention. An active member of the Toltec tradition, he has lived with the

---

*Lew Welch, quoted by Elizabeth Powers and Elias Amidon, *Earth Prayers* (New York: HarperCollins, 1991).

Wirrarika Indians of Mexico, the Lacandon people in the rain forest of Chiapas, and the Nahuas in the mountains of Puebla. He shared this walk with me for the first time as we were hiking to the top of Ajusco Mountain, which is one of the circle of mountains surrounding Mexico City. After only an hour or so of really focusing my attention on the Count Three practice of walking, I was astounded by what I saw and understood how much I was missing by walking in my usual way. My awareness and perception were awakened to a whole new way of experiencing walking.

The Count Three walk is an effective exercise to divert your attention from your everyday world and refocus it on the world in which you are traveling. After the usual familiarization period, its effects will be immediate. It basically involves acknowledging three things in front of you with each step you take. In doing this your mind does not have time to think about its usual worries and concerns and must relinquish control to the attention necessary to acknowledge or "count" these three things every time you step.

When it finally does surrender control in this way, you will have opened yourself, through conscious counting, to discovering the energy of all the specific elements surrounding you. This will help you not only to become intimately familiar with your surroundings (you will learn untold things about the wildlife, flora, insects, and other living beings in your immediate area) but also to become connected in a very deep rather than superficial way with your environment. You may discover something about the area's history by spotting fossils, animal bones, old structures, and so forth and you may learn about the land itself—whether there has been a fire in recent years, or maybe a flood or drought.

A number of factors can affect your experience, such as the season in which you walk. Everything in nature—animals, plants, trees—adjusts with the seasons in ways that go beyond those small changes that occur every day. No two Count Three walks are ever the same—even when they are performed in the same place. The observations you can make are limitless and the wonders and discoveries you will find along your path will raise your attention to new levels whenever and wherever you walk in the future.

Instructions for the Practice

1. Begin with the Fox Stance.

2. With each step, as you look at the ground directly in front of you, count three things you see. For example, while I step with my right foot I might see a small twig, then an oak leaf, then another oak leaf. With the left step I see a small brown rock, then an acorn, then a tiny white flower. With the next step I notice a leaf, then the remains of a mouse, then an owl feather . . . and so on. If it's helpful, you can number aloud the things you see with each step.

3. Continue for at least a half hour, but the best results will occur with sustained walks of one to two hours.

Comments on the Practice

Remember that this activity is completely new to your attention and it won't be easy at first. Don't become discouraged if it seems difficult in the beginning, and don't worry about having a speedy list with each step. Though in the examples given above I have named what might be seen as you walk, in your actual practice don't try to announce by name—even silently—those things you notice. It's almost impossible and indeed unnecessary to name each thing that you see as you fully acknowledge it and maintain a reasonable walking pace. Simply *acknowledging fully* each item and moving on to the next is the best goal.

To receive the maximum benefit from this walk, do it in a forested area or in any region that has diverse vegetation. But please don't interpret this too literally—some areas such as high-altitude deserts may look rather barren in some seasons until you actually begin your walk and discover how much there really is to see and learn there.

Sometimes I incorporate this walk into a longer hike or as a part of a set of Earthwalks to be practiced during a day of wilderness walking.

7. Count Three Variation

*It was on these walks that "something" started shifting inside. . . .
Something from nature reached out, grabbed hold of me, entered
my being . . . I began hearing birds, tuning into their songs. They
sang to me as I walked along the trails. I began hearing the colors
of the leaves, tasting the smell of the air, feeling the changing
seasons. My senses came alive in new and different ways.*

LESLIE IRENE SHORE*

In Walk 6, Count Three, your attention remains focused on the ground in front of you, but with this practice you will be looking ahead at eye level or slightly higher to allow your view to open and you to see an entirely different picture, even if you walk the same route as that taken for Count Three.

Instructions for the Practice

1. Follow the instructions for Count Three, but be sure your head is positioned to enable you to see straight in front of you at eye level or, in some moments, even a little higher.

2. It's fine to move your head slightly from left to right as you note three things with each step, but try to keep the position of your gaze straight ahead as much as possible. It's natural, for example, to follow for a moment the path of a bird that flies

---

*Leslie Irene Shore, *Healing the Feminine: Reclaiming Woman's Voice* (St. Paul, Minn.: Llewellyn Publications, 1995).

across your field of vision. But try to avoid jerking your head in a different direction every time something catches your eye on either side of you. See how much you can discover by looking forward all the time.

Comments on the Practice

As similar as it seems to Count Three, the Count Three Variation does have some distinct differences. The position of your head and your view above the ground dramatically alter the complexion of the walk. I suggest starting with the Count Three and then, as your skill level increases, trying this variation. For beginners the Count Three makes for a more effective way to enter the magic of attention than the Count Three Variation because keeping your attention focused on the ground is less customary than looking straight ahead. In addition, because it may seem to us that there is less to look at on the ground, it actually takes much more attention to repeatedly count three things on the ground than three things at eye level.

As you walk, remember that if your attention is occupied with noticing items in front of you several feet off the ground, then you really will not be able to watch exactly where you are stepping—be careful not to trip, but also be careful not to destroy any plant or animal life in your path.

8. Walk of Silence

While you are here, connect to Earth Mother. Your life experience requires this. If you want to influence your life experience, you need to appeal to the Mother of the child. The harmony we sing with Her occurs in the space of silence. And the song we sing is the song of experience.

BLACKWOLF*

---

*Blackwolf Jones and Gina Jones, *Listen to the Drum: Blackwolf Shares His Medicine* (Salt Lake City: Commune-A-Key, 1995).

Converting your ears into radar and your whole energetic being into a giant antenna is the goal of this walk. You move through the world like a shadow, silent, not really touching anything, but present nonetheless. Your feet make no sound, your breathing is so shallow that you can barely hear it yourself. You move with agility, grace, and precision—absolutely silently. Does this sound impossible? Give it a try.

Instructions for the Practice

1. Start in the Fox Stance and begin Walk 1, Walk of Attention—except this time, move without making a single sound. This will require that your hearing becomes the center of your attention. Try not to step directly on dead branches or dry leaves or brush up against anything that will produce a noise. If you are walking in a forest, you will probably have to move at a very slow pace, which will require patience, determination, enormous focus on where you place your feet, and the ability to anticipate the sounds you will make as you travel through the environment.

2. Here are some hints on technique: Try to step without touching your heels to the ground—minimize the area of ground that your feet actually touch and you will minimize the sound your feet produce. Try to keep your balance and center of gravity on your rear foot. Commit your weight to your front foot only at the exact moment when your back foot leaves the ground. By doing this, your walk will resemble more a floating motion than a usual walking gait. By "floating" through the natural world in this way you will be amazed at how much more wildlife you can see, how much more silence you will "hear," how many more new sounds you will discover, and how much greater the level of connection to your surroundings will be.

Comments on the Practice

Don't be discouraged if your progress is slow. It takes time to move silently in Nature—it's a big challenge even for people with extensive experience walking in the wilderness. The rewards of learning this Earthwalk are many—the time and patience it requires are well worth it. I've found that one of the best rewards is being able to see the expressions on the faces of animals—they will be initially surprised to see you because most humans can be heard long before they are close enough to be seen. But then, as they slowly recognize that you are walking as they themselves do, they will begin to accept your presence. This will provide you with a precious glimpse of a world that lies hidden to most people.

Another reward of walking in silence is the chance to learn the language of nature. Actively trying not to make noise enables you to hear birds talking and singing, the sounds of wind in the leaves, the music of water flowing. Try to understand what you hear. If you are not quite quiet enough, the blue jay will make a particular set of noises to warn his companions that you are near—and the squirrels and deer will sometimes do the same. If, however, you hear the consistent pecking of a woodpecker, you know you have been silent enough—this sound is usually a signal to the other animals of the forest that all is well. Listen to the sound of water to tell how close it might be, or to the gusts of wind that might tell you that a change of weather is on the way.

9. Night Vision

Just as the interior world of our psychological experience has many qualities that are ambiguous and indeterminate, so the external world now discloses its own indeterminacy and subjectivity—its own interiority, so to speak. Perception, then,

is simply the communion and deep communication between
our own intelligence and the creativity that surrounds us.

DAVID ABRAM*

When night falls, the world changes. Twilight ushers in the forces of night, the animals of the world change their habits and patterns, and the moon and stars rule the sky in place of the sun. It is a time of mystery when discoveries are waiting to be made. We limit ourselves to the world of light by always chasing away darkness, and in doing so we miss this mystery and the chance to explore our inner abilities and sensory gifts.

Because we now have electric lights to eliminate the darkness, we seldom allow ourselves the chance to explore the dark world. For most people it is an automatic action to turn on the lights when they enter a dark room or to turn on a floodlight or carry a flashlight when they walk into their yard at night. When we get into the car, a light comes on automatically—indeed, many people program lights in all of their environments to come on automatically whenever darkness arrives.

With this Earthwalk you will embrace the darkness, become one with it, and explore its mysteries and secrets. Most of us think that we can't see in the dark, but this isn't exactly true—we simply have forgotten how to do it. Granted we'll never see as well as, say, an owl or other night creature, but the point is to learn that we limit our experience of the natural world's magic and our full range of sensory gifts by limiting ourselves to the world of light.

It's important to first note that rarely are we confronted with the absolute absence of light, and this is especially true outdoors. The ability to see in the absence of normal levels of light is something that develops with practice and requires letting go of your preconceived notions regarding your limitations. Believing that you can successfully attain your goals is the first step to achieving

*David Abram, "The Perceptual Implications of Gaia," in Allan Hunt Badiner, ed., *Dharma Gaia* (Berkeley: Parallax Press, 1990).

them and this belief is absolutely necessary to adopt when performing the walking practices in this book.

There are a few techniques that you can use to draw out and develop your night vision. Try using a part of your eye that's different from what you usually use. Don't take this too literally—of course, the physiology of seeing always remains the same. Instead, alter your attention: Concentrate on your sight emanating from a place just behind your eyes. This will seem strange at first but can be developed to a high degree and is a valuable tool that taps into our hidden abilities for increased vision in darkness.

Another technique that may be helpful is to feel as though you are becoming a creature of the night—a raccoon, fox, skunk, or cat, for example. Animals that function comfortably primarily at night are perfect models for our pursuit of night vision. Emulating the movements of a night creature such as a fox or a cat can help you to enter into the darkness with comfort, poise, and increased self-assurance, which will, in turn, allow you to relax and make friends with the darkness.

Give yourself time to get used to how things appear in darkness. Then, focus your attention just as you would in the light in order to increase your ability to notice and perceive all the elements of the natural world, from animal scat to an owl in a nearby tree. You may find this is easier than you anticipated—we are automatically more alert and attentive in the dark precisely because of its shadows and mystery.

Finally, it is helpful to look directly into the darkest places when you walk in darkness. This goes against our natural instinct to look toward the light, but looking directly at the darkest areas makes the areas around them appear lighter. It also challenges you to meet head-on the task you are engaging in, instead of looking for the easiest way out.

You can first practice this walk when the moon is full but the experience is its richest when the moon is new.

Instructions for the Practice

1. Beginning in the Fox Stance, close your eyes and simply breathe for a few moments.

2. Open your eyes and begin to walk silently, using the "floating" techniques learned in Walk 8, Walk of Silence: Step with your heels barely touching the ground, keep your balance and center of gravity on your rear foot, and commit your weight to your front foot only at the exact moment when your back foot leaves the ground.

3. Begin using the sight from "behind" your eyes while envisioning yourself as an animal of the night. Walk carefully and stealthily and embrace the darkness as your friend and companion. Peer into the darkest areas around you and, imagining the sight coming from behind your eyes, see what is there. You are in a super alert state and every part of your being is attentive, even your hair and skin. Pay close attention to what is on the ground in front of you and what is overhead.

Comments on the Practice

Over time, as you become comfortable and familiar with moving in the darkness, you will find it more difficult to find areas that are truly dark. At this point, in order to derive the greatest enjoyment from this walk, you will have to perform it as far from a city's lights as is safely possible in addition to choosing nights that have particularly heavy cloud cover or very little moonlight. If you are walking in a remote area, take friends along with you. This company can even add to your experience.

As a being of the night, welcome your cousins the skunk and the owl, and invite them to join you. Show them that you can be as alert, observant, and silent as they are.

Even in the night there are plenty of shadows—try to see what lives in them, and instead of avoiding them, try walking directly within them.

The beings of the night are highly attentive, and to become one of them you will have to be extremely quiet in your movements. Use all that you have learned in the Walk of Silence and enter the night with silent awareness. Through practice you will develop your ability to the point at which merely "seeing" becomes "perceiving" in the dark. At this point you will actually seek out opportunities to relish the darkness.

10. Walking Backward

So, friends, every day do something that won't compute . . . As soon as the generals and politicos can predict the motions of your mind, lose it. Leave it as a sign to mark the false trail, the way you didn't go. Be like the fox who makes more trails than necessary, some in the wrong direction.

WENDELL BERRY*

Walking backward is an exercise with the power to stop the flow of your view of the world and start it moving in a whole new direction. Far from being silly, versions of this walking practice have been and still are used in many cultures and disciplines throughout the world to help change a person's perception and perspective of the world both externally and internally. The potential for someone else to see you as you perform it can challenge your ego as well.

Additionally, it allows you to feel your body in a whole new way. Your sense of balance and equilibrium are challenged, your visual perception of the world is altered—things recede instead of advancing toward you, and all of your senses are heightened to compensate for the significant perceptual changes you experience. As with many of these Earthwalks, the effects of walking

---

*Wendell Berry, quoted in Elizabeth Powers and Elias Amidon, *Earth Prayers* (New York: HarperCollins, 1991).

backward are cumulative—the more time spent practicing it, the better the results.

Instructions for the Practice

1. Begin in the Fox Stance, but distribute your weight slightly forward (over your knees) instead of over your back foot.

2. Remember that the key to even weight distribution is not committing your weight to one foot until the other leaves the ground. This allows you to be ready to shift your foot placement at the last moment should you have to due to an obstruction in your path, the need to avoid stepping on a plant or animal, and so forth. Most people shift their weight mid-step, resulting in their weight distribution swinging back and forth as they walk. The backward translation of this is that the ball of the foot crashes to the ground first with the weight leaning back, followed by the heel hitting the ground. In this backward walk especially, try to concentrate as your weight shifts from one foot to the other and try to complete this motion as smoothly and fluidly as you can, because a result of not being able to see exactly where you are going might be that you'll need to change the direction or length of your stride at any moment. In addition, remember not to lean back, which is to say for this walk, do not lean in the direction you are walking.

3. While walking backward, you should be looking at the ground directly under your feet and using your peripheral vision to help you navigate. Indeed, you will be amazed at how much you can see by using your peripheral vision.

4. As you walk, feel first with your lead foot, then step. In fact, your most important guides as you travel will be your lead foot and your sense of touch. You must feel with your lead foot what you are going to step on before you commit your weight to that

foot. For example, if you are walking backward on a sidewalk and feel soft grass beneath your lead foot instead of concrete, you will know that you have strayed off course. In the woods your lead foot may feel a fallen log or a large rock in your path, allowing you to adjust accordingly.

Comments on the Practice

Your first consideration is safety. Walking backward can be a blind nightmare or it can be a safe and enlightening experience. Performing this practice correctly will reduce your chances of tripping and falling down, and even if you do fall will make for a much softer landing.

Once you have become accustomed to walking backward, your timidity will lessen. Enjoy this practice for at least a half hour, noticing the new feeling in different muscle groups and tuning in to your change in perception. Note especially how reversing your perspective 180 degrees could affect the habits of your everyday life.

The easiest place to begin learning this walk is on a running or walking path or on a baseball or football field—anywhere, in fact, where you feel completely relaxed about the path beneath your feet. In the beginning, knowing that there is nothing behind you or beneath you that you might trip over allows you to concentrate on what is at either side of you. After developing your peripheral vision and the ability to use your lead foot as your main tool to tell you where you are going, you can challenge yourself further by walking backward in a variety of environments. Do not perform this walk where there is apparent danger; areas where there are steep and/or rocky trails, quarries, or any ground that falls away suddenly should be avoided.

11. Hat with Mirrors

One day ... I had the shocking realization that I had just
walked for about ten minutes without having said a single
word to myself. ... My entire thought processes had stopped
and I had felt I was practically suspended, floating.

Carlos Castaneda*

This practice was developed in the AVP workshops from inspiration provided by the writing of Carlos Castaneda, whose character Pablito, through his experiments with different activities to break up the continuity of the everyday world, comes up with the idea of a wooden helmet with mirrors attached that allow him to see behind him as he walks backward.† *Continuity*, while itself not a negative concept, becomes negative if it consists of the viewpoint and values currently held by our society, which often undermine the goal of reconnecting with the spirit of Nature.

I have to admit that the first time I heard of this walk I wasn't too inspired to try it, but having practiced it for many years, I now feel it is a remarkable exercise that has many benefits, not the least of which is the sense of fun it imparts.

This practice involves walking backward outdoors with the aid of two mirrors mounted to your hat—rearview mirrors—that help you navigate. After a good deal of practice you will be able to use the mirrors to walk backward with the same speed and ease with which you walk forward. The unusual combination of skills and perception that are required for this walk work to develop attention in specific ways. With continued practice, it will be possible to merge your attention to the view behind you in the mirrors with the

---

*Carlos Castaneda, *Tales of Power* (New York: Pocket Books / Washington Square Press, 1974).

†Carlos Castaneda, *The Eagle's Gift* (New York: Pocket Books/Washingon Square Press, 1981).

view you have in front of you. This results in a 360-degree field of vision and a kind of attention that can quiet the mind.

Like other walks in this section (but in a more novel fashion), this walk asks that you concentrate your attention, both mental and physical, on an activity that is foreign to your everyday world. According to usual standards, this activity has no tangible reward and, therefore, no value—and this is precisely the reason for doing it. In order to break the spell of a world gone mad and restore our bond with Earth, we must look past conventional values and modes of perceiving. Entering into this activity with your whole mind and body allows your attention to be saturated with actions that don't support the industrialized world's view of reality—you are, in effect, walking away from all things commercial or industry controlled or mainstream—and opens you to a flood of sensory information so new that you have no room for thoughts of the "outside" or familiar world. Simply the willingness to perform this walk indicates that you are aware of the need to change and that you are, as psychologist Chellis Glendinning so aptly phrases it, "in recovery from western civilization."

When I perform this walk or other activities that don't fit within the norm and am confronted by people who clearly find my actions or appearance unusual, I simply repeat Glendinning's words—that I'm in recovery from contemporary civilization—and announce that my activity is part of my "intervention therapy." My observers either ask to join in or walk away, shaking their heads!

Instructions for the Practice

1. The hat with mirrors can be made very easily: Use any hat with a brim in front (baseball hats work well) and two bicycle mirrors (already equipped with a mounting arm that should be flexible so they can be adjusted)—those with a diameter of three to five inches work best. Mount the two mirrors on the front of your hat so they are at eye level and six to ten inches apart. To

do this, put on your hat and position the arm of one mirror on the brim, moving it until you find the best location for viewing behind you. Mark where the hole at the end of the arm meets the brim. Repeat this process for the second mirror and then cut out two small holes in the hat brim—no larger than the width of a small screw or nail—where you have made the marks.

Bicycle mirrors usually come with mounting hardware (screws and nuts)—if yours don't, you'll have to buy them separately. Mount each of the mirrors by matching the hole at the end of the arm with the hole in the brim, inserting the screw through both the arm and the hole, then securing the screw with a washer (optional) and the nut. If you are not mechanically inclined or have trouble with this procedure, you may have to ask a friend for help. Be sure to try on the hat during the mounting process, adjusting the mirrors up and down and side to side as necessary until they allow a full view of the area behind you. I usually adjust the mirrors so that I can see for reference my ear and the top of my shoulder in the inside edge of each—much as you would adjust your car's side mirror to include a bit of the car for reference.

2. To begin your walk, choose a location similar to the one used for Walk 10, Walking Backward. As your skill develops, you can move on to locations with more difficult terrain. Once you are walking, concentrate on what you see through the mirrors alone. This will give you confidence in your ability to use the mirrors to guide you as you move.

3. When you feel comfortable, shift your attention so that you are viewing at the same time the area you can see in the mirrors and the area in front of you. This will result in a significant perceptual transformation. From this point you will essentially be viewing the world from a 360-degree field of vision while

walking backward. Give yourself time to bask in this entirely new perspective—it is best to perform the walk for at least a half hour. An interesting and challenging variation is to perform Hat with Mirrors at night.

Comments on the Practice

Please don't give up when you first try to make your hat with mirrors! For years I was unable to enjoy this walk because I couldn't get past my frustration the first time I tried to make the hat. It was only when someone gave me a completed hat that I was able to try it—and I couldn't believe what I had been missing! Note that it is important to find mirrors with flexible arms—it makes adjusting them much easier.

Remember to walk slowly and smoothly, as in Walk 3, Walk of Equilibrium, so that your head isn't bobbing up and down. If your head bobs, the mirrors will bob, which will make them quite useless. At first, pick an item behind you, such as a tree, and walk toward it, moving your head from side to side to get the feel of using the mirrors. When you approach the tree, practice walking past it on both the right and the left in order to learn how to convert to the spatial the visual message of each mirror. You might try using just one mirror and gradually begin to incorporate the other. In the beginning you might also try adjusting one mirror to view straight behind you and the other to view the ground. I also point one mirror up sometimes, so that I can look into the trees or sky, which affords an especially good view at night.

12. Five Steps

Still round the corner there may wait
A new road or a single gate;
And though I oft have passed them by,
A day will come at last when I
Shall take the hidden paths that run
West of the Moon, East of the Sun.

J.R.R. TOLKIEN*

This Earthwalk will increase your sensitivity to the fact that our view of what is ahead of us can change with just a single step. I am often astounded that no matter how many times I have walked the same trail, I discover I missed other trails that branch off from it, or that along the path there were places of beauty I never recognized before! This same thing happens in our everyday lives as well. How many opportunities do we simply not see because we are too busy with what we are doing, are in too much of a hurry, or are steadfastly clinging to a single point of view? The world is a place of opportunities and hidden joy waiting to be discovered. Walk with open eyes and take a moment to pause and see what is happening around you. Discover how to walk without passing things by.

Instructions for the Practice

1. Begin outdoors in a place that can be either familiar to you or brand new. Position yourself in the Fox Stance and perform Walk 1, Walk of Attention, for a few minutes until you are relaxed and your thoughts are quiet.

2. When your body tells you that you are ready, stop walking and close your eyes. Take a few deep breaths and listen for thirty

---

*J. R. R. Tolkien, *The Lord of the Rings*, collector's edition (Boston: Houghton Mifflin, 1965).

seconds to one minute, then open your eyes and look around. *Really* look and see what surrounds you, on the ground, on the horizon, and above you. Now listen intently to all the sounds surrounding you—pick them out and isolate them one by one. Then smell the scents and isolate them. Draw in the energy of the place and feel its unique ambience. Take your time.

3. Now slowly take five steps forward, stop, and repeat step 2. Don't close your eyes this time unless you feel the need—simply observe the new scene in front of you using all your senses and energy.

4. Continue in this way, noticing how many things can happen, appear, and change within five steps.

Comments on the Practice

You can spend anywhere from thirty seconds to many minutes observing in between each set of five steps. You can even vary the duration from set to set depending upon how you feel. But don't rush. Hurrying along will take the magic from the walk.

This style of walking is used by many alert animals in the natural world—and each of them is rarely caught unawares. My two favorite teachers of walking, the mountain deer and the fox, will rarely walk more than a few steps without surveying the entire scene around them. If you are walking on terrain that is relatively unchanging over a large area, then it will be quite a challenge at first to notice and observe differences in your surroundings every five steps—but this challenge is the point of the exercise. If you remain disciplined and take only five steps at a time, you will begin to learn the lessons that our aware cousins the deer, the fox, and the bear already know; you will notice treasures that would otherwise remain hidden from you.

Experiment with this Earthwalk in the context of your daily life—many of its lessons are the same whether you walk in the woods or in the city.

13. Shadow World

If we pull the shadows out from the background, if we give them shape and density—a presence of their own . . . the hidden and shadow places become real, the perception of depth emerges into consciousness and, if for only a moment, the world is reversed.

LAURA SEWALL*

When we look at the world through the remarkable gift of sight our eyes provide for us, we are experiencing the visual version of reality. Our sight allows us visually to identify and subsequently name all of the things around us. The sense of sight enables us to enjoy all sorts of colors and shapes, objects, and expressions of creativity and natural wonder.

But while we are enjoying all that we see, we are missing a world right in front of us because we have learned to see in a specific way—we focus our visual attention on colors, patterns, and light. When we look at the scenery around us, we are drawn to the light objects and to whatever physically moves. Darker shadows exist to add depth and contrast, and variations in the quality of the light add mood and clarity.

However, there exists an entirely different way of viewing the world, one that requires looking into the shadows cast by the objects around us. This way of seeing opens the door to the shadow world, where a whole new awareness and perception of reality exists.

When we view the world in this way we are training our perception in a manner that is the opposite of what we have taught it in the past. This allows us to break from our usual perception of the world so often based on what is in the light and what is rational. In truth, the side of darkness is just as valid and the night is as important as the day.

Laura Sewall, *Sight and Sensibility: The Ecopsychology of Perception* (New York: Tarcher/Penguin, 1999).

The world of shadows is simply the complement to the world of objects. We can learn to use this other world to help us shift our perception, silence our thoughts, and expand our view of the world.

This Earthwalk begins outdoors, usually during the early morning or late in the day, when the shadows are longest and when the worlds of night and day mingle.

Instructions for the Practice

1. Assume the Fox Stance, close your eyes, and breathe.

2. Open your eyes and focus softly on the shadows, allowing the darkness formed from light hitting objects to become the dominant focus of your visual attention. You are not trying to eliminate the objects in the light, but instead are allowing them to become the elements that add depth and contrast to the scene just as the shadows do when you see the world in the usual way.

3. Close your eyes for a moment and open them again. Establishing a connection with the dark through closing your eyes will help you to more readily see shadows as the predominant part of a scene.

4. Start to walk while viewing the shadows. Whenever you have trouble sustaining this perspective, close your eyes for a few seconds. Begin to peer into the shadows as you walk to see what is there. To remain connected to the shadow world, you must look in a "soft" way and you must combine this with looking at specific things around you—at the shadows on the undersides of leaves; the shadows behind rocks and trees, among tree branches, and on the ground; and the shadows created by animals and birds. Notice the energy of the shadows and the beings that live in that cool darkness. Leave behind your rational mind and open up to a world you have never experienced before. If you see a magnificent shadow tree or shadow being that is arresting, then stop walking and look at it, studying it for as long as you wish.

Comments on the Practice

Once you learn this technique, you will see wondrous things. Animals know how to use the shadow world and Nature flows in the world of shadow as well as light. Be alert to what is happening in this world and you will cross over into new areas of perception and awareness.

Remember that you can apply the lessons of perceiving the shadow world to your life beyond this walk. Looking at your everyday world while consciously moving to the foreground what lies in the background can be good medicine for Earth. The causes of many of the crises she now faces stand in the background, the quiet yet consistent habits of modern people.

14. Into the Unknown

Each moment of existence conditions the next, but there is no abiding subject that binds all these moments together. . . . All things in their very depth are in a state of flux. . . . The dance of impermanence extends beyond the physical world to the mind and states of consciousness. Consciousness itself is impermanent. To reach the state where there is no becoming, one must accept that everything, absolutely everything, is always becoming.

ELIZABETH ROBERTS*

The vast majority of the tasks we engage in day to day make use of predominantly one sense—sight. Almost everything we do involves seeing. To be temporarily deprived of sight can give you a clear picture of how much we rely on it—and how much we are capable of doing without it. Walking without the use of sight—even in the most familiar places—takes patience, courage, and the use of all your faculties and other senses. Carrying the practice to more

---

*Elizabeth Roberts, "Gaian Buddhism," in Allan Hunt Badiner, ed., *Dharma Gaia* (Berkeley: Parallax Press, 1990).

difficult terrain, a forested area, perhaps, will require you to move beyond your perceived limitations and tap into feelings and intuitions that connect you with your surroundings on an energetic level. Most important in this Earthwalk is to let the person you think you are fall away so as to open yourself to the reality that exists beyond the confines of thought or intellect. Only when you are truly ready to challenge all levels of your being should you engage in this particular walking practice.

Instructions for the Practice

1. Find a partner who can walk in front of you and act as your guide and choose a walking place with flat terrain that is free of obstructions.

2. Tie a blindfold—a scarf or bandanna—over your eyes so that you can't see.

3. Assume the Fox Stance and lightly place your hand on the leader's shoulder. You won't be leaning on your leader, but rather walking behind him at arm's length.

4. Begin to walk in tandem with the leader, switching hands if your arm becomes weary. As you grow more comfortable trusting your partner and walking in this way, begin noticing the sounds, scents, and feelings that are enhanced when your sight is unavailable.

5. Next, when you have grown comfortable with your new awareness, let go of your leader's shoulder. It's important to keep your arms and hands in their Fox Stance positions rather than following what may be instinct and throwing them straight out in front of you in fear, which, along with making your lower body more vulnerable to injury, is detrimental to your balance. Bend your knees and continue walking attentively. Relax and embrace the darkness, make friends with it.

6. Your leader's role has now been redefined—rather than leading you physically, he leads you with sound by walking in a way that is just loud enough for you to hear. The noise that your leader produces will depend on the type of terrain you have underfoot. If it is gravel or stone, then a simple shuffling walk would produce sufficient sound for you to hear him and follow. On grass or any other surface that is inherently quiet, your leader may have to stamp a bit as he walks so that you can locate him. It's important at this stage that your leader maintain a pace that you can comfortably match.

7. A word about safety: Your leader's challenge will be to constantly observe you and your surroundings to ensure your safety without allowing this concern to detract from the walk. Partnering in this walk, then, requires a large amount of attention and creativity on the leader's part, and a large amount of trust and attention on the part of the blindfolded follower. For example, if there is a fallen log in your path, one thing your partner might do is tap the top of the log with his foot as he passes over it. If you are listening closely, you will hear the tap, assess the sound for its location, and be able to feel the log carefully with your foot as you step over it. If the log is higher from the ground, your partner might decide to tap it with his hands, which will produce a completely different sound. Careful listening and experience with this Earthwalk will help you deduce that the obstacle is higher from the ground.

Comments on the Practice

Mastering this practice will take time and experimentation but you will be amazed at how fast you learn and how quickly your other senses compensate for your missing sight. Allow your other senses and your intuition to take control. Feel the warmth on your skin when you walk in the sunlight and the coolness of the shade. Be aware of the breeze with your amplified senses of hearing and smell. In fact, try to hear and smell all you can while you walk. Using the senses that usually take a backseat to your sense of sight can feed your intuition—and this increased intuition can be a wonderful resource to you even after you return to the world of sight.

Those who have advanced beyond the beginner stage can apply their skills to difficult terrain. Winding trails, uneven ground or ground covered with fallen trees or rocks, paths with steep or changing grades, and wet areas provide unique challenges for walking without sight. Just remember to move slowly, use your best walking form to maintain balance and equilibrium, and, most important, develop with your partner a system based on rapport and trust. Ultimately this Earthwalk is an exercise for both of you, and the greatest learning will occur if you trade places often. Working with the same partner(s) over time will invariably produce the best results.

As your confidence level and attention increase and you tackle more difficult terrain, you'll start to trust your interaction with your surroundings at a level close to the trust you experience when you have your sight. This is significant on a physical and practical level and also serves as a reflection of your shift in attitude and perspective. When you allow yourself the opportunity to work without the use of your sight, you are embracing the unknown. You are sending a clear signal to yourself and to the world that you are not afraid and in fact are willing to face the unknown head on. While this attitude may have been foreign to you up to now, it is indicative of strength and courage and shows a commitment to self-improvement and the idea that sometimes we see more when we wear a blindfold.

15. The Beacon

The body can function as a perceiver in ways that will not necessarily agree with what we consider to be the ordinary way to perceive through the senses.

VICTOR SANCHEZ*

This practice, which involves covering your eyes as you walk through a large open space with the guidance of a partner, is an excellent exercise for raising your awareness level and increasing your confidence as you walk without sight. Its level of safety makes it a wonderful exercise for children as well, allowing them to encounter and explore the full use of their other senses in a way that puts their mind very much at ease because of the minimal risk and self-determination involved—all they need to do to see again is remove their hands or the blindfold. The only drawback to this practice is that by minimizing the risk, you allow for the possibility of not fully using all your attention. Because of this, your intention and the manner in which you enter into the walk are extremely important.

An additional factor in this exercise is pace, or speed. The depth of experience that you are able to achieve does not have to correspond to the pace of your walk, but in this practice you have the opportunity to walk fast or even run into the great mystery that surrounds us. Through my experiences in AVP workshops I have had the pleasure of witnessing hundreds of people employing a version of this technique with remarkable results, and it is one of my favorite Earthwalks relating to attention.

Instructions for the Practice

1. With a partner, find a large open space free of obstacles or obstructions. A sports field or large area of lawn is perfect.

---

*Victor Sanchez, *The Teachings of Don Carlos: Practical Applications of the Works of Carlos Castaneda* (Santa Fe: Bear & Company, 1995).

2. Cover your eyes with your hands or with a blindfold and have your partner position himself far away from you.

3. Your partner should begin to make a sound that will call your attention to his location. This call can be a sound made by the voice, a drum, or whatever you like as long as it is loud enough for you to hear.

4. Begin walking in the direction of the call. There is no talking involved—the "caller" will use exclusively the sound of the call (unless you are about to hit some obstacle, in which case he may simply say "right" or "left" or simply "stop.") Continue walking until you reach the caller and he says "stop." The impulse to slow down or even stop altogether when you are aware of getting close to the caller is quite common—but don't. Continue walking until the caller's voice signals you to stop. It is the responsibility of the caller to do this at the appropriate moment, especially if you are performing this practice while walking fast or running.

5. Once you are comfortable, begin experimenting with some variations: Switch roles; or have the caller move around the area so the walker's destination is less distinct; or vary your pace as you walk.

Comments on the Practice

The sound the caller is making is your beacon in the darkness. Sometimes, when you have fully entered an entirely different awareness, it becomes quite easy to get "lost," to lose connection to the world you are most familiar with. Whatever happens during the exercise, this beacon is your connection to the world you know. During this practice you must continue to be aware of the presence of the caller so that you can react to any direction he may give if you are at risk. Likewise, it is important that the caller give directional signals that correctly correspond to your position—for instance, a call of "right" should mean the walker's right, not the caller's. Of course, any signals given by the caller should be as brief as possible.

This practice has always been a favorite of workshop participants because it can produce dramatic shifts of awareness for those who allow themselves the freedom to explore it fully. Be aware that during and after this type of experience it is not uncommon to feel very deep emotions—a direct result of how rarely we allow ourselves to touch the hidden parts of our awareness.

Fully embracing this walk will successfully separate you from the rational part of your mind and the voice that you listen to in your daily life. Becoming in tune with the other parts of your awareness is necessary to living in balance.

16. Embracing the Darkness

I do not know if you have ever noticed that when you give total attention there is complete silence. And in that attention there is no frontier, there is no center, as the "me" who is aware or attentive.

J. KRISHNAMURTI*

After you have become fully adept at Walks 14 and 15, Into the Unknown and The Beacon, it's time to try walking alone without sight, a practice that requires using all the other senses at a high level and following strict guidelines for safety. It is best to begin this practice with a partner present though not involved. This provides you with the opportunity to explore your environment safely. This is the only Earthwalk for which indoor and outdoor practice is suggested.

---

* J. Krishnamurti, *Meditations* (Boston: Shambhala, 1979).

Instructions for the Practice

1. With your partner watching, cover your eyes and simply let your feet take you where they may. Engage your sense of direction, feel the different energies of the rooms or areas where you are walking, sense when you are approaching a wall or tree or other obstacle. You will find that the body has the ability to feel in many ways—most of which are quite different from those we are accustomed to in our visually driven world. Note that your partner should speak only when it is necessary for safety.

2. Once you have developed some proficiency, you can begin to assign yourself specific routes to a particular destination such as a certain tree on a trail or a specific room in your house, trying to arrive at these places without coming in contact with anything.

Comments on the Practice

Remember that this is not an exercise of memorization emphasizing your recall of the placement of certain objects in a room or area, but rather is focused on developing that unnamed part of yourself that *feels* what is around you. This part of you is confused and hampered by visual and tactile clues. Try to reach a level where you don't need to see with your eyes or feel with your hands to know exactly where you are. Be sure to reduce the possible risks of injury before you start.

Learning to navigate in the darkness in this way can endow you with a profound sense of confidence in your ability to navigate the problems and challenges that present themselves in life. While the trials and unknowns in life can sometimes feel overwhelming, embracing the darkness allows you to expand your possibilities and possible resolutions.

As you walk, remember to use common sense, take care of your body, and embrace the darkness.

17. Predator and Prey

*The animal envoys of the Unseen Power no longer serve, as in
primeval times, to teach and guide mankind. Bears, lions, elephants,
ibexes, and gazelles are in cages in our zoos. Man is no longer the
newcomer in a world of unexplored plains and forests. Neither in
body nor mind do we inhabit the world of those hunting races of the
Paleolithic millennia, to whose lives and life ways we nevertheless
owe the very forms of our bodies and structures of our minds.
Memories of their animal envoys still must sleep, somehow, within
us; for they wake a little and stir when we venture into wilderness.*

JOSEPH CAMPBELL*

The relationship between predator and prey embodies one of
Nature's ever-present cycles. Our lack of connection to our food
sources, our domestication of animals, and our desire to live in
temperature-controlled environments have sufficiently removed
us from the natural world's cycles to such an extent that most people
in developed countries go through their entire lives without ever
witnessing the process of predator seeking prey. While there are
certainly animals that eat mostly plants, a large number eat other
animals, all of them links in the great food chain of Nature—and
we ourselves are the final, uppermost link, choosing which plants
and animals are most profitable and convenient to exploit and raise
for our own food. Of course, there are people who eat only plants,
but they are part of the cycle as well—even animals at the top of
the food chain are prey for the Great Huntress, death, who makes
all things equal and returns everything to Earth to begin the cycle
again.

This should not be perceived as a morbid concept—the cycle
of life and death and the behavior of predator and prey are inter-

---

*Joseph Campbell, *The Power of Myth* (New York: Doubleday, 1988).

woven in the balance of life on Earth. Awareness of the one sure moment that will come in your life—death—can give your life strength and immediacy. An animal's predatory skills—hunting and survival skills—make him what he is. The smartest, strongest, and most alert survive. Animals develop abilities and grow strong and knowledgeable while trying to evade predators and live to see another day.

In this respect, humans have become weak. Our modern pursuits have advanced us in other areas but at the cost of our *wildness* and abilities pertaining to survival in the world of the wilderness.

In this walk you will delve into both sides of the predator/prey relationship and discover and explore skills and feelings that are inherent in both roles—what it feels like to be engaged in the covert search for prey and what it feels like to be aware that just around the bend you might find yourself being hunted by a larger or more skillful predator. For this walk it is best to locate yourself in an area of wilderness that is full of animal life. A forest in the nonwinter months is ideal.

Instructions for the Practice

1. This practice begins the moment you enter the woods. Start walking very slowly as you would for Walk 8, Walk of Silence. As you travel, transform your perception into that of a predator hunting the woods with skill and precision. You notice everything that moves, everything that breathes, and you notice every shape and color and pattern that surrounds you. You move silently, keeping your own sounds to a bare minimum while you listen attentively for any sound of prey—a slight rustling on the ground or signals in the air that clue you to its presence. Feel with all of your senses and intuition what is happening around you as you continue to walk slowly through the wilderness.

2. The moment you see or hear a living being, it becomes your prey. Avoid being seen or heard by your prey as you approach it.

Crouch behind trees or bushes, time your movements to coincide with the wind or other sounds. Continue feeling like a stalking predator. As soon as you see your prey, it is yours—there is no need to try to catch it; simply get as close to it as you can and then move on to your next target.

Continue in this way for at least a half hour, exploring deeply this experience of being a skilled predator.

3. Next, switch your focus to becoming the prey of something infinitely stronger and smarter than you. Feel at the core of your being that you are suddenly being watched. There is something out there that is highly skilled and deadly silent, and it is after you. Notice every sound around you, see every movement in the environment as a potential threat.

4. Continue walking with this feeling—where is your pursuer hiding, from which direction is it coming? Try to walk in a way that your hunter can't predict. Be calm but super-aware. Use everything available to you to conceal yourself as you walk. Walk in the shadows, hide momentarily behind trees or bushes, at times walk while crouching low to the ground—and watch everything around and above you. It is no good to stop moving; you must keep walking or you will be caught.

Explore this feeling of being the prey for at least a half hour.

5. To end the walk, try exploring the feelings of being both predator and prey at the same time. This is the state that most wildlife experience all the time: the endless pursuit of food coupled with the threat of becoming food at any instant. Explore this duality deeply while walking in the wilderness and you will better understand the cycles of life in the natural world.

Comments on the Practice

There are many ways to enhance the experience of this walk. One way might be to imagine you are a specific animal. For example, if you are walking as the predator and you see a squirrel, you might try imagining yourself as a cat or a bird of prey such as a hawk. Moving with a sense of yourself as a particular predator of the animal world can help you to feel a more immediate connection to such an existence. Or, by contrast, you might imagine yourself as a mouse being hunted by an owl or fox.

It's important to open yourself to allowing the actual environment of your walk— the sounds, movements, colors, textures, shadows, and smells—to enhance the reality of your experience in such a way that you, in your assumed roles, can enter into the life of the world around you.

18. Cure for Loneliness

The greatest delight that the fields and woods minister is the suggestion of the relationship between human beings and the natural world. I am not alone and unacknowledged. The trees and plants nod to me and I to them. The waving of the boughs in the storm is new to me and old. It takes me by surprise, and yet is not unknown. Its effect is like that of a higher thought or a better emotion coming over me, when I deemed I was thinking justly or doing right. Yet it is certain that the power to produce this delight does not reside in Nature alone, nor in humanity by itself, but in a harmony of both. . . . Nature always wears the colors of the spirit.

RALPH WALDO EMERSON*

A number of years after I began to work with groups of people in workshop settings, I one day found myself feeling very lonely. It wasn't a strange feeling—I'd had the feeling of loneliness many times throughout my life. But this time it was different because it

---

*Ralph Waldo Emerson, quoted in Anne Rowthorn, *Earth and All the Stars* (Novato, Calif.: New World Library, 2000).

came during a period in my life when I seemed to have no reason to be lonely. I was truly feeling very happy about the path I was walking, and because of my close friendship with the AVP instructors and the hundreds of people I had met and become friends with through workshops, I had more people in my life whom I truly loved than I had ever had before. I told my friend Victor how I was feeling and without hesitation he said to me, "Jim, go out into your woods and don't come back until you find your answer. I'm sure you'll be back very soon."

So off I went into the woods, actually feeling a bit annoyed at Victor's reply. I was hoping for an answer from him, not a suggestion for what I could do. But after walking for a while, I found myself relaxing and enjoying the serenity of the wilderness and the familiarity of that place. As I traveled, I asked myself why I was feeling so lonely until I saw an old tree that I knew well—and then I asked him. As I stared at the tree, I noticed a chipmunk looking down at me from the branches, and above him was a robin. I watched them for a while and because I heard no answers from my friend the tree, I continued on my way.

A few moments later I was startled as a large fish leaped from the river next to my path, making a splash as it landed back in the water. I waved hello to him and kept walking until I reached a meadow. Just as I waded into it a red-tailed hawk flew out of a tree on the other side of the expanse of grass and began its upward circle of flight. I watched the hawk as I walked until I stepped on something hard beneath my feet. I looked down and there was a turtle! I apologized, but he was already inside his house and didn't seem to be interested in coming out.

After a few more minutes had passed, the hawk was nowhere to be found. Feeling a little disappointed at losing sight of the bird, I sat down in the tall grass and asked myself again why I felt so alone. Contemplating this and feeling sorry for myself, I fell asleep.

Sometime later I awoke with the feeling that something was

crawling on me and when I looked I found that it was a deer tick looking for a nice place to have a meal! I removed him, slowly sat up, and peered out through the tall grass. I will never forget what I witnessed: life—everywhere life, all around me, surrounding me. Everywhere I looked I saw a living being! I saw trees and birds. I saw grass and flowers and plants. There were three deer walking at the far end of the meadow against the border of the woods. In the grass and in the air all around me were insects, large and small. In a flash I recalled the old tree I had seen earlier, the chipmunk, the robin, the fish, the hawk, and the turtle. And then it was clear to me: How could I possibly feel alone? How could I possibly be so self-absorbed and self-centered? Who could possibly feel alone in a world filled with so many wonderful and magical beings?

Then I knew the answer to my question—feeling disconnected from all this could leave a person feeling very lonely, and with all my work to involve myself with helping others, I had become disconnected.

I shook my head and laughed at myself then, and as I started walking home, I felt all the living beings around me were laughing too. What Victor had said was right—I had found my answer in the world I knew best.

I haven't forgotten this lesson, and so whenever I feel lonely I go for a walk in the wilderness and try to reconnect with the flow of the natural world. When you are feeling lonely, try this simple Earthwalk.

Instructions for the Practice

1. Begin walking outdoors. As you walk, take a few deep breaths. Notice and take in all the life surrounding you—see each being, each plant, flower, tree, insect, animal, bird, and human. Feel how everything contains the magic of life, including yourself. Listen deeply to the sounds of life on the ground, in the trees, in the air. Smell, taste, and explore the sensation of sharing this

life with all the beings around you and with all the beings on this marvelous Earth.

2. After you have taken in this world, tell yourself that you are not alone. Everything, including you, is connected in the web of life energy that surrounds us every moment of our lives. Walk with this understanding inside your heart.

Comments on the Practice

It's no small wonder that intentionally placing ourselves in the world of Nature can be a cure for loneliness. For thousands of years our human species has been in intimate contact with all the living beings of our natural environment. As hunter-gatherers for much of our time here, we were just as much a part of Nature's workings and cycles as everything living around us. In acknowledging this, prominent psychologists and biologists refer to a hidden awareness deep within us that they term the *ecological self* or the *world self.* Two-time Pulitzer Prize–winning science professor Edward Wilson uses the term *biophilia* to refer to our innate emotional affiliation to other life-forms on a genetic level. Whatever you choose to call it, both our physical and sacred connections to Nature are undeniable, and through them the natural world is always there for us when we need her most.

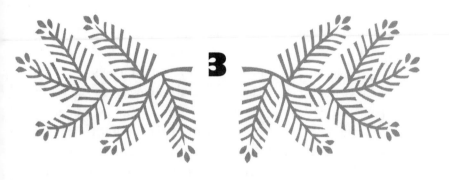

Walks for Groups

A GROUP

Although most of the Earthwalks included in this book can be performed by more than one person at the same time, the three walks in this section are specifically designed for the purpose of creating companionship and cooperation among those in a group—including children—while at the same time fostering a healthy and enjoyable interaction with the natural world.

These walks, like those I introduced in the last section, promote the active engagement of our attention through a medium wholly separate from our language-based learning process that leads to knowledge of ourselves and the world around us. But along with promoting connection to ourselves and the world, these walks also encourage both a physical and an energetic connection to other human beings that is refreshingly devoid of the games of domination that we so often play and free from the masks we so often wear to hide our vulnerabilities and insecurities.

These practices allow you to share an energy and spirit with those who walk with you and create an opportunity for discovery and personal interaction that is rarely present during the hustle and bustle of our daily lives. To take time out to join together with friends, family, or even complete strangers, and, in an intentional way, learn to notice and enjoy both Earth and the company of other human beings, is to create a space for magic, love, and a real understanding of one another's strengths and weaknesses in ways that go beyond words.

For many years I have been walking in this way in places all over the world with small groups of five people to large groups of more than eighty. All of these practices have been beautiful and powerful gifts to my life, and I hope that they will be for yours as well.

19. Walking as One

[We] create one another, depend on one another, are literally part of one another, our land passes in and out of our bodies just as our bodies pass in and out of the land, that as we and our land are part of one another, so all who are living as neighbors here, human and plant and animal, are part of one another, and so cannot possibly flourish alone.

WENDELL BERRY*

When a group of individuals form and maintain a single line while walking, they make of themselves a single body that can go much farther than its separate parts. The energy of individuals is melded and transformed to such an extent that the walkers are united and moving in a different world that can't be perceived using normal attention.

During this Earthwalk I have witnessed hundreds of people explore hidden parts of themselves and discover facets of attention and perception that they never knew existed. When performed by a group of people familiar with the walk and its key elements, it is not uncommon for the group to enter into a separate reality. Time, emotions, worries, obligations, concerns all slip away and are replaced with tranquillity, unconditional love, and a sense of freedom and joy. The walk's destination is an internal one: a level of connection within the group that allows each individual to feel the group as a single unit. This walk has changed my life in many ways. From the first time I experienced it many years ago right up to today when I practice it with my companions in the mountains, it has provided the gift of sharing time with people and Nature at once. This sharing brings everything together—and the world transforms.

---

*Wendell Berry, *Clearing* (New York: Harcourt Brace Jovanovich, 1977).

Instructions for the Practice

1. Your group—two or more people—stands single file. Each of you is positioned in the Fox Stance, with the left foot forward. The distance between each person in the line should be a little more than arm's length. Maintaining this space is important both to maintaining the combined energy of the group and for challenging your attention: If this distance between people increases at any one place in the line, then the connection between members of the group will be severed and the walk will lose its force. Constantly maintaining this arm's-length space, however—especially as you walk over difficult terrain—requires high levels of attention. As it grows easier for you to keep this spacing, challenge yourself to walk even closer than arm's length from each other.

2. As you walk, step at the exact same moment as the person in front of you, and with the same foot. This involves much more than simply marching. Concentrate at such a level that at the exact moment when his or her toe hits the ground, your toe hits the ground; when his or her weight shifts, your weight shifts; and when his or her opposite foot lifts off the ground, yours lifts off the ground.

3. In areas where the terrain is flat and smooth, it will be easier to create a kind of rhythm together. However, moving through a forested area or over rocky, uneven terrain becomes much more challenging. Matching the step of the person in front of you when walking over fallen logs or up and down steep hills requires a great deal of attention. It's important to remember to be patient with yourself and the person in front of you or behind you and to realize that the rewards are well worth the work. If you fall out of step with the person in front of you, pause for a half second until he or she takes the next step—then you can get back in sync. Allow yourself to flow easily with the

walk and enter into the magic of the time. Many people I know who practice this walk actually try to position themselves behind someone who is inexperienced so that they will be even more challenged. Now that's the proper attitude!

4. Keep your hands free as you walk; if you need to carry anything with you, use a backpack. Adopt a finger/hand position that is unusual for you—a loose fist, perhaps, or maybe two fingers open and the rest curled under. Whatever you choose, it's important that your hands are not simply flailing as you move— it's best that they're in a position requiring attention to sustain so that you'll have one more focus to help quiet your thoughts. Feel free to change the position of your fingers once in a while if you are walking for long periods. As you practice, assuming a hand position will become natural.

5. Regulate your breathing to the rhythm of your walking. Breathing fully and correctly is an art form that has been tragically lost to people in the modern world. Breath is life, and the way we breathe can give us insight into how we live and help us lead better lives. While there exist many specialized forms of breathing, for this walk you should be concerned simply with being aware of how you are breathing, doing so in a way that helps you flow and connect your energy to the walk. This awareness of your breath will help you to adjust it to the rhythm of your step.

6. Walk in silence. Only if you need to say something should you call out "stop" and then give the group your message. Relating to each other in a way that is not language based is a central theme of this Earthwalk; you will have plenty of time to talk when you have finished walking. On some occasions, when your group has attained a high level of cohesiveness, the power of the place where you are walking might give all of you a song, inspiring you to share it together out loud. If this happens, don't resist: Let its joy—or sorrow—fill you. (Sometimes the places

where you walk will inspire sadness if they bear the signs of our disregard for Nature, such as scattered trash, scarred trees, and insensitive and hurtful development.) However, such occasions are rare and special—it is best to remain silent unless you clearly feel the impulse to do otherwise.

7. Keep your vision trained on the person in front of you—specifically on his or her feet. Every time you lift your eyes from the feet of the person in front of you, you break the continuity of the group, risk falling out of step, and disturb the delicate state of awareness you have cultivated up to that point. Each time you look up, it's like starting the walk all over again. There will naturally be someone at the head of the line. This person should be a trustworthy leader so that the others are confident they'll not get lost or find themselves in danger and thus feel little compulsion to look around as they walk. The leader's responsibility translates into a slightly different practice. He or she will need to choose a path based on the interest of the group as a whole. To do this, the leader practices the Walk of Attention while noting how his or her walk may affect the others behind. Through practice, doing this will become quite natural.

8. Keep your attention focused on the elements of the walk and not on your thoughts. The reason this walk is so effective at cultivating attention and knitting together the group is that your mind, occupied with a number of tasks at once, doesn't have room to think. But this is true only when you focus fully on the elements of the walk. Sometimes even when you are trying hard to remain focused, the little voice inside your head will continue to ramble. If this is the case, don't fight it—the best thing to do is simply to treat it as if it were one more sound among all the other sounds around you, no more important and no less important. Just let it blend and mix right in. It's not possible to simply tell yourself to turn off the voice, but if you focus on what you're doing, it will not have the power to bother you.

9. As you walk, feel the presence of the others in your group and use the elements of the walk to move past the limits of your individual ego so that you can merge with them and the natural world.

Comments on the Practice

When first performing this walk, try to include no more than ten people in your group—especially if the leader is unfamiliar with the practice. After you have grown comfortable with the technique, the number of walkers who can participate is unlimited.

Since this walk involves a group of people, it is important to be aware of the impact you will have on the area where you are walking. Be respectful of all the living things in your path. The leader of the walk has the responsibility to navigate in a way that reduces as much as possible the harm to plants and animals that live where you are traveling. Being conscious of this will further your connection to the energy of the area.

It is especially important to this walk that you not place your attention on where you are going. The magic of your journey functions on a purely internal level. The place you want to reach is a place of energetic connection where the awareness and attention of the group merges to form an experience more powerful than one that is achieved individually. This merging of individual energy into something greater is still a familiar practice among the indigenous people with whom I have walked. Single-file walking techniques are most often performed by these people during long trips, such as pilgrimages to sacred sites, which might involve walking for months at a time. Even though groups making such trips do have a specific destination in mind, they trust that they will arrive at the appropriate time and walk in the "now" and as a single unit. An added benefit is that the sick, weak, or tired in the group are helped both directly and at an energetic level by the rest of the group.

The levels of energy and attention that can be reached by a group walking in this manner for weeks or months at a time are astounding.

It is common knowledge to people who live near the destinations of Huichol Indian pilgrimages that groups of pilgrims can walk by in single file without ever being seen or heard. The energy of such groups is transformed to such an extent that they are, in effect, walking in a world that those with usual attention cannot perceive.

20. One Body

When we contemplate the whole globe . . . flying through space with all the other stars, all singing and shining together as one, the whole universe appears as an infinite storm of beauty. This grand show is eternal.

JOHN MUIR*

This is an extremely potent Earthwalk combining many of the aspects of Walk 19, Walking as One, with the mystery and perceptual shifts that accompany walking without sight. The results are extreme shifts of awareness and perception—in the realm of walks that can be performed by groups of people, it is one of the most powerful.

Its effects are accomplished through many elements. The first is lack of sight, which opens the door to perceiving without visual interference. The next is the fusion of the energy of the people in the group, resulting in an energetic body that is much larger in size and much more diverse than any individual energy field. This concentration of energy allows the entire group to attain a deep level of perception and silence in a relatively short period of time. Finally, in the realm of sightless walks, this one provides the added security of moving in a group, which can help those who are blindfolded to relax more easily and release more readily the control of the rational mind, which can lead to the opening of doors of perception that might otherwise remain closed.

---

*John Muir, Sierra Club exhibit on John Muir, electronic file, www.sierraclub.org.

This walk is a lesson in inner balance and control, as most walks that involve groups are, which translates into being able to move outside your ego and resist becoming angry, upset, or disappointed when the person in front of you or in back of you does something potentially distracting to you.

I can sum up the rewards of this walk in three lines:

When I have nothing, I am free.
When my body is empty, I feel.
When I close my eyes, I see.

Instructions for the Practice

1. This walk requires a responsible guide who is not blindfolded and a walking area that is relatively flat and free of obstacles. Begin by assembling a single-file line with each person standing, left foot forward, one arm's length from the person ahead of him or her. The leader, who is not blindfolded, is at the front of the line. If the group is big, you might consider incorporating one or two additional people without blindfolds whose job it will be to ensure the safety of the walkers and to remove any small obstacles from their path.

2. Each person should tie on a blindfold and then gently hold onto one shoulder of the person in front of him or her. Be careful not to grab tightly or lean on your person.

   As soon as everyone is blindfolded and in position, talking should cease. Before moving, take a few moments to breathe, relax, and embrace the darkness and the wonderful mystery surrounding you.

3. Begin walking slowly. As with Walk 19, Walking as One, anyone experiencing a problem during the walk should call out "stop," at which point the leader or helpers will resolve the problem and indicate when the group can begin moving again.

4. It is important in this walk that the group travel continuously for a long period of time—at least one hour. During this time the leader can explore with the group different speeds or turns and circles. Any change in pace or direction, however, should be smooth and slow to create the least amount of distraction and confusion. The leader has the privilege and duty to help his companions in this walk and should carry it out responsibly, with the needs and benefit of the group in mind.

Comments on the Practice

Be aware that as you follow this practice, two forces will become apparent to you. The first is the force of your rational mind holding you back from embracing the mystery, trying to remain in control as you pursue the "risky" activity of walking blindfolded. The other force is your other self who craves the excitement of breaking free from this physical and rational world and yearns to express itself. This Earthwalk offers the chance to do just that. We do not often enough give our other side a chance to emerge—make the most of this time and let go of your rational mind. There will be plenty of time after the walk is over for it to take over again.

21. Together

We are in this together. Never before have our destinies been so intertwined. The fact that our fate is a common fate has tremendous implications. It means that in facing it together openly and humbly, we rediscover our interconnectedness in the web of life. From that rediscovery spring courage, a deeper sense of community, and insights into our power and creativity. . . . The affirmations . . . can be explained in terms of systems theory, psychology, and spiritual teachings, but their truth for us who engage in the work comes from what we experience together.

Joanna Macy and Molly Young Brown[*]

---

[*]Joanna Macy and Molly Young Brown, *Coming Back to Life: Practices to Reconnect Our Lives, Our World* (Gabriola Island, BC, Canada: New Society Publishers, 1998).

This group, blindfolded walk to be performed by two or more people is at the end of this section for several reasons. It is difficult, challenging participants on many levels and requiring the absolute attention and concentration that can lead all of you to a state transcending attention, a state of silent awareness of the movement of energy among you. It also requires extreme patience and discipline in order to avoid becoming frustrated with yourself and your companions. But the reward is well worth the effort— success with this practice indicates that you have acquired not only the ability to walk in physical balance but also the ability to access your extrasensory awareness.

This walk should be learned in an open area that is free of obstacles, such as a sports field. When proficiency increases, you may challenge yourself by moving to more difficult terrain.

Instructions for the Practice

1. Each participant will need a bandanna or scarf and the group as a whole will need a piece of thin rope the length of which will be determined by the number of walkers. This walk is performed much the same as the previous two walks, beginning with a single-file line, but instead of each walker holding onto the shoulder of the person in front of him or her, all of the walkers are tied together, beginning with the leader, who wraps the rope around his or her waist, and continuing with each member of the group until all members have the rope wrapped twice around their waists with an arm's length of rope between each person.

2. The leader's eyes remained uncovered, but all other participants tie on their bandannas or scarves as blindfolds. The walkers position themselves in such a way that the rope between each of them is taut without pulling on the person in front or behind.

3. With a signal from the leader, the group begins to move. The challenge is to neither walk too quickly so that you run into the

person in front of you nor cause the person in front of you to tug at the rope because you walk too slowly. You must keep a consistent rope-length distance between you and the people in front and in back of you for the duration of the walk. To do this, try to be attentive to the sounds and movements of the person in front of you, but also strive to reach a higher level of awareness with your feelings and senses, which will result in knowing the location of that person, yourself, and the person behind you. When all the members of the group attain this level of awareness, the group will have formed an energetic connection that defies our normal boundaries of awareness and perception.

4. Continue walking in this way for at least one hour.

Comments on the Practice

Don't attempt this walk unless all the members of the group are proficient at the previous walks in this section. Even then it may not be possible to successfully perform this because it requires such highly attuned energetic awareness. Remember that you can always come back to this practice after completing the rest of the walks in this book, thereby giving yourself the opportunity to hone your energetic awareness even further. Despite its difficulty, this practice is great fun and a challenge even for the best walkers I know. Don't be frustrated if you can't do it right away. It takes hard work and strong intention.

More than any other walk, this one demonstrates that we are all connected in this life on Earth. The rope in this walk represents this connection. Through it each of us can cooperate with others to move forward, be pulled along by others, or become angry and, perhaps, stop altogether. Whichever action you take will affect all those around you.

Walks of Connection to the Powers of Earth

NIERIKAS

Now we move our attention to walks that develop a personal relationship with and connection to the powers of Nature that are available to us if we simply learn their language. Reestablishing this connection can strengthen your life and awaken your personal relationship to Earth, making for a magical journey that actually feels in many ways like returning to your real home, to the place where all your relations live.

Through my work and experiences with both the surviving Toltecs (specifically the Huichol Indians of Mexico) and the new Toltecs, I have had the good fortune to actively enter into the world of Nature and not merely observe it. This participatory experience consists of a real exchange of energy—a bodily conversation with something that is much bigger than you but at the same time lives inside of you. The resulting deep feeling and knowing connects you intimately to the flow and rhythm of the life that animates all the beings of this world.

To better define what this section of the book involves, I'd like to borrow a word from the language of the Huichol—*nierika* (pronounced nee-er-ee-ka). *Nierika* has many meanings—"vision," "clarity," "mirror," "doorway," "essence," and "power" among them. We will use the word here in a way that somehow wraps up all these meanings together. An example would serve best to explain this: When you walk on the beach, the ocean beside you is such an incredible force and source of life and power that you can feel it immediately. This feeling is part of the *nierika* of Water, which, along with Fire, Earth, Sun, and Wind, is one of the five main powers that affect the lives of all of us. Nierikas can also be felt at sacred sights as well as in places such as canyons, lakes, springs, and mountains.

Feeling the nierika of a particular stream or mountain or power of Nature—such as Fire—might lead you to give a name to that entity or power, just as the Huichol and many other indigenous groups do. Doing so is a way of personalizing your relationship with a power, of entering into a stronger personal exchange with it. The Huichol have hundreds of names for the multitude of natural powers familiar to them. Fire is named Tatewari, and it is the oldest power. His nierika can enlighten and connect us to the vast knowledge of the universe.

Remember, however, that naming these powers does not lead to immediate understanding; too often we believe we know something simply because we can name it. I invite you instead to think of the name of each nierika simply as a means of evoking its mystery and magic. Even though the Huichol have names for all five main nierikas, because these Earthwalks are meant for all people no matter what their background, I will use their English names here—Fire, Earth, Sun, Wind, and Water—and leave to you the possibility of naming them for yourself.

It is one of the ironies of our industrialized society that harnessing the physical power of the nierikas to run our machines and homes is one of the reasons we have lost touch with their sacred gifts to our lives. While these Earthwalks are certainly not the only means of reconnecting to the nierikas and their true offerings, they are extremely effective in providing the kind of activity that encourages interaction with Earth as a whole and the nierikas specifically. It is important to remember that the nierikas are already aware of us. They are inside us and all around us; they are a part of everything that forms our world. Performing these Earthwalks is simply a way of offering yourself in the spirit of likeness to everything around you. If you open your heart to receive the knowledge or support of the nierikas, then you can bring this magic home to your life in a way that expresses their unconditional love, strength, and beauty.

WIND

From the moment we draw our first breath on this planet we are blessed with the life-sustaining power of the nierika of Wind. Every moment we are alive she is a part of us, moving in and out of the deepest regions of our bodies, enriching our blood, and helping to sustain every living thing around us. In currents and layers she moves through the upper regions of our world, caressing and shaping it and, with grace and power, blowing life into all newborn beings. At times menacing and lethal and at times soft and refreshing, she is ever present, whether or not we are aware of her.

Wind is alive. Anyone who understands her only as a by-product of differing air pressures hasn't yet discovered her essence. Wind has the power to communicate, cleanse, heal, and change our direction. Connecting in a practical way to this nierika can reveal important aspects of ourselves and our world. She gives movement and action to everything, making the trees strong and the leaves fall. We breathe her in and she sustains our life. As she moves in endless currents she tirelessly animates branches, grasses, and flowers, and sweeps clean the rocks, soil, and atmosphere. Touching all things at once, Wind brings us the gift of communication. Traveling effortlessly through our world, she carries messages, news, omens, and gifts of all kinds, in all languages. Sounds, odors, tastes, energy patterns, and feelings flow from her with their messages of joy, fear, power, and tenderness. Moving energy from the five main powers through all beings while touching everything at once, Wind can help us to see our lives with the breath of freedom. Placing ourselves in a position to be cleansed by her is a beautiful and proactive way of connecting to her nierika.

We will work with Wind first because the practices connecting us to her are accessible and powerful as we begin to learn from all the nierikas. The lessons and insights gained here can be applied as we continue to even more challenging aspects of walking this sacred path of connection.

22. Communication

Air is a matrix that joins all life together. . . . In everyday life we absorb atoms from the air that were once part of birds and trees and snakes and worms, because all aerobic forms of life share that same air. . . . The longer each of us lives, the greater likelihood that we will absorb atoms that were once part of Joan of Arc and Jesus Christ, of Neanderthal people and woolly mammoths. As we have breathed in our forebears, so our grandchildren and their grandchildren will take us in with their breath.

DAVID SUZUKI*

Touching all things at once, Wind, or air, serves as a sacred vehicle of information for all the beings in the world of Nature, including humans. Learning to communicate with it opens you to discover what is happening around you, what has happened in the past, and how you communicate with yourself and those around you.

This Earthwalk will help you to discover the Wind nierika in a tangible and practical way. You can alter the physical form of the walk to correspond with any physical manifestations of Wind and the corresponding sensations these call up within you. For example, if she is at your back, you may feel her pushing you and subsequently "let go" of your body in deference to Wind's desire to take you to a special place. Or you may feel Wind blowing her gentle breath upon you and you may raise your palms to receive her and allow her to flow through your whole being. There might even be times when you use Wind's power as a bird does, lifting your arms

---

*David Suzuki, *The Sacred Balance: Rediscovering Our Place in Nature* (Vancouver: Greystone Books, 1997).

like wings to transform your walk into a dancing flight. Allow yourself to communicate in the form of thoughts and feelings but then translate these into movement as you walk.

I take a moment here to remind you again to please be safe with your physical body. It is only a container and can be broken if your attention becomes separate from your intention, leading to carelessness or, perhaps, recklessness.

Instructions for the Practice

1. Locate yourself in a natural setting that is free from the distractions of other people. It might be best, especially at first, to perform this walk on a day that is breezy or in a location where Wind's presence is most noticeable.

2. As you begin to walk, become aware of the air entering you and leaving by way of your breath. Become aware of what this gift means to you and to your life.

3. Shift your attention to the air's presence all around you and note that it moves into and out of all the living things within your sight.

4. As you continue walking, begin to listen to Wind's expression by its sounds as it moves through, over, around, and under everything around you. Focus your attention on how sounds, odors, tastes, and other sensations are delivered to you by the movement of the air.

5. Begin to let Wind express herself through the movement of your body. There are no rules for this—you can move your body any way that feels right in the moment. Engage in a dialogue with Wind at the level of your body, opening yourself to whatever comes in, listening with every part of your being and then expressing what you've heard with your movement and voice. Run, talk, dance, shout, laugh, cry, walk fast or slow, walk low

to the ground or on your tiptoes, walk backward or sideways as you allow Wind to walk through you.

6. Notice how your body feels as you move and bring to mind how you communicate with it. Do you listen to it? At what level? How about the people in your life—do you listen to them? How do you respond to them? What our your habits of communication? Try and discover from Wind how to communicate with honesty and strength, with softness and gentleness.

7. Walk in this manner for at least forty-five minutes and then, as you near the end of your walk, ask the Wind nierika a question about your life. Listen, feel, and watch for a message or answer, but don't expect it to come in a predictable way. Observe and remain attentive to the movements of your body and of everything around you and to the feelings and perceptions that flow into you as a result of the wind's currents and shifts.

Comments on the Practice

The word *spirit* has developed from the Latin *spiritus*, meaning "breath." Just as *spirit* connotes the sacred, so our air, this life-giving breath all around us, is sacred. Through the element of air there is a continuous communication among all the beings and life systems on the planet. The spirit of Earth also communicates with us through the Wind (air) nierika. When we learn to listen, we can hear the words of Earth and all life and grow closer to both.

23. Cleansing

O Great Spirit of the North,
invisible spirits of the air,
and of the fresh, cool winds . . .
From you comes clarity and strength,
and the power to hear inner sounds,

to sweep out old patterns,
and bring challenge and change . . .
for the good of this planet Earth,
and all living beings upon it.

RALPH METZNER*

By opening ourselves to the cleansing power of Wind we allow her to blow fresh life-inspiring air into every part of our energetic body. She has the power to help us remove our social masks, cleanse ourselves of physical and emotional baggage, and find that the essence of our being can be so much more beautiful than the outward projections we manifest in order to cope with a chaotic world.

Although not a prerequisite, this practice is most successful when performed without clothing. You will have to gauge weather and the level of privacy available to you to determine if this is possible. It is also preferable to perform this walk on a windy day.

Instructions for the Practice

1. As you begin to walk, notice how Wind tirelessly forms and shapes the natural world. Feel her essence entering into every part of your body, even through the pores of your skin.

2. Feel the wind blowing right through you, cleansing you of all negative emotions and all the toxins you have accumulated within from daily life in the modern world. Turn as you walk, exposing every part of yourself to the wind, and breathe deeply in and out to help this process of cleansing.

3. Speak or even shout your intention to be cleansed of those things in your heart that you wish to be free from. Be specific—speak names, describe events.

   As you walk, feel these things blowing away from your body

---

*Ralph Metzner, *Green Psychology: Transforming Our Relationship to the Earth* (Rochester, Vt.: Park Street Press, 1999).

and melting into the enormity of Wind's power as though they never existed.

4. Before finishing your walk, express your thanks to Wind for helping you on your path.

Comments on the Practice

Remember that it is perfectly fine to let your body move in whatever way Wind inspires it—even if this means stopping for a few moments as your experience unfolds. Indeed, perhaps the place where you stop is significant to your experience.

Be open to the possibility that there may be a certain quality of the wind or a certain strength in its flow where you are walking that resonates particularly well with you and leads you to very specific and unique feelings. The depth of cleansing you receive from Wind during this walk is determined only by how effective you allow it to be. While this cleansing occurs at an energetic level, the physical aspects of the walk help you to feel its effects more deeply.

A strong wind will probably help you embrace this walk more fully, but it can be performed with only a light breeze as well. In the case of lighter wind, your senses must be used fully and in a focused way in order to experience completely the physical sensation of cleansing.

Like being infused with the warmth of the sun or washed with the freshness of water, being caressed by Wind as it blows over your skin and through your hair is a magical experience that can help, heal, and renew.

24. Changing Direction

[As a sailboat] we must take into count the currents—which are our own unconscious motivations, our desires and emotions, our patterns of actions. . . . The winds that fill our sails are the forces of time and climate and season; the tides of the planets,

*the moon, and the sun. Sometimes all the forces are with us; we
simply open our sail and run before the wind. At other times,
the wind may run against the current, or both run counter to
our direction, and we may be forced to tack
back and forth, or furl the sail and wait.*

STARHAWK*

We are constantly in a state of motion. As fields of energy, we move through life in an ever-changing state of being and because of this magical fact we have an incredible facility to adapt if we need to or want to. We sometimes get stuck in energetic patterns, however, and sometimes forces keep us from the creative motion necessary to live the energetically healthy life that our inner being craves. This is a condition that is unfortunately extremely common and very harmful to our energetic body. The good news is that many powerful techniques can be employed to break free from this trap, and working with the power of the Wind nierika is one way.

Wind can move with such energetic force and intention that if we had never felt it, it would be impossible to imagine. As she helps Earth move through her cycles of life and death, it is not difficult to be witness to her power. She can easily cut through man-made constructions; she can move unfathomable amounts of water wherever she desires; and she can gently deliver life-giving seeds and pollens to the bosom of Earth where they can begin to grow. In short, she tirelessly provides invisible forces of motion that sustain the energetic movement of the world.

It is a simple thing for Wind both physically and energetically to move a comparatively small energy field like you—but in order for this to be possible, you must first get the attention of her power by developing your relationship with her through your actions and by stating your intention on an energetic level.

---

*Starhawk, *The Spiral Dance: A Rebirth of the Ancient Religion of the Great Goddess* (New York: HarperSan Francisco, 1979).

This walk uses the power of Wind to help you make a shift in direction in the way that you use your energy. This change can be small, pertaining to a specific item in or aspect of your current life, or it can be dramatic, encompassing your entire being. Again, as in previous walks, intention serves as the guiding force of your connection. Although this practice has specific steps, its effectiveness lies largely in the areas of energy and intention. Ultimately, your actual experience is dictated by the nierika of Wind herself.

It is ideal to perform this walk in an area relatively free from obstacles and where the wind is strong. An area that is high and exposed or a flat windy plain is a good example of suitable terrain.

Instructions for the Practice

1. Begin performing Walk 1, Walk of Attention, to help quiet your thoughts, and continue until you start to feel a connection to Wind.

2. As you feel the force of the wind, fully notice its direction. Focus on this direction for a few minutes and then turn to explore the other three directions. For example, if you begin walking with the wind at your back, turn and thoroughly explore walking with the wind coming directly at you and then to either side of you.

3. Next, stop walking, close your eyes, and, standing in place, slowly turn in circles as you ask Wind to help change your direction of energy as it relates to a specific life situation or your overall path in life. Fully and energetically offer your situation for her to see. The more specific you are, the better the result will be.

4. Continue spinning slowly until you feel compelled to stop. Don't allow your rational mind to enter this process and tell you to stop at a certain point. Feel with all your being the direction of the wind as it comes at you. This is your new direction in this moment.

5. After you've stopped turning in place, open your eyes and begin to walk in whichever direction Wind takes you. Feel the energy of this new direction and explore it thoroughly.

6. As this part of the process comes to a close, turn and face Wind and thank her for helping you.

Comments on the Practice

Remember that this is not a directional change corresponding to the points on a compass. The term *direction* here is simply a way to describe how your energy is flowing. The actual direction from which the wind is blowing in terms of north, south, east, and west might even be the same at the end of your walk as it was at the beginning. This is not important. What is of value is that you have placed in Wind's power the direction of your energy so that she can help you change the direction of your energy flow.

SUN

The Sun nierika is the most powerful source of energy in our world. There is nothing around us that he does not influence, and Earth responds to his energy in countless miraculous ways. As he spreads light and energy—the life-giving forces of our existence—throughout the solar system, he connects us and the essence of every being on our planet to the rest of the universe. Because all the beings on our planet are composed of this brilliant, luminous energy, we are all brothers and sisters. Sun is our true father, the very beginning for all of us.

While many of us take Sun for granted because he appears every day, it is easy to witness the reverence given him by other beings of Earth simply by looking around—trees and plants grow toward him to feel his loving energy, flowers open at his request, and fruit ripens under his watchful eye. Animals bathe in his warmth, welcome his return in the morning with songs of delight, and howl in appreciation as he lights up our moon.

To connect to the energy of Sun on a personal level is to realize the pure magic that surrounds us every moment of life. The daily miracles produced as a result of Sun's efforts are intimately intertwined with the cycle of creation and death. Recognizing and celebrating the elemental role he plays in our lives can place your perspective of the world and your life in a realm where the trivial aspects of living in modern society are shown for what they really are: insignificant pieces of the game that we use to pacify our burning desire for a more authentic life. Selfishness, anger, jealousy, and materialism all seem pointless when we look into the sky and see the face of our true father shining his energy onto us and bringing the light of hope and the miracle of life to everything he touches. As human beings we can join with the other beings of the planet to celebrate every day the gifts he bestows.

25. Sunrise

Dawn and sunset are mystical moments of the diurnal cycle, the moments when the numinous dimension of the universe reveals itself with special intimacy. Individually and in their relations with each other these are moments when the high meaning of existence is experienced.

Thomas Berry*

The moment the sun's first rays shoot over the horizon to meet a new morning is a magical time of transformation—the world moves from dark to light—and marks the birth of a day. Nocturnal creatures go to their daytime sanctuaries while all other beings awaken. Thus the cycle and the balance of the natural world continue.

Sunrise marks the coming of light and energy to the world for another day. The nierika of Sun at sunrise has been honored and used by humans for ages, and the first appearance of this nierika after a period of darkness is the perfect occasion to connect with and absorb this power, which can result in an experience that, although it defies description, is ultimately energizing, healing, and life changing.

I will never forget my first true moment of connection to Sun. I was high up in the Sangre de Cristo Mountains of Colorado and I had just spent an almost sleepless night alone huddled under a tree. I was in the middle of an unconventional version of a vision quest that required me to be without anything except the bare essentials for survival. I had water but little else—no food, shelter, or fire, and for warmth only one small blanket and the clothes I wore. I had

---

*Thomas Berry, *The Great Work: Our Way into the Future* (New York: Bell Tower, 1999).

been fasting for only two days, but a long, cold, night had left me feeling depleted, and when finally I saw the first hint of the dawn coming, I immediately stood up and faced east. Standing there shivering in the dark and cold, I reviewed the happenings of my night—the sounds, thoughts, emotions, dreams, and, of course, the shivering. I could begin to see the glow of the sun behind and the mountain in front of me. As the ambient light increased I was anticipating seeing at any moment the sun rising from behind the peak. I waited for what seemed an eternity, shaking out my legs, blowing warm breath onto my hands, and staring intently east in anticipation.

And then suddenly it happened. The first ray of light from the rising sun shot out from behind the mountain and pierced my heart. It was like a long thin beam of multicolored light that, when it touched me, felt like a gift of immeasurable magnificence and splendor. It was at once impersonal and filled with enormous love. The next thing I remember is watching the glowing disk rising swiftly into the sky and the warmth of its rays entering my entire body. Spontaneously I raised my palms to catch the rays and began walking toward him in this way. As the orb continued rising, I began to walk faster and faster until all cold and sleepiness were thrown aside—and as I gradually began to slow my pace, I started to sing a song that came from somewhere deep inside me, a melody and words that I had never heard before but seemed to have known all my life. I sang words of thanks and joy, receiving the rays of the sun into the palms of my hands and then rubbing my palms all over my body. Sun infused me, an empty vessel, with his nierika and at that moment I was a little Sun shining on Earth. For the first time I truly intuited my sacred connection to this nierika and in that suspended moment I was filled with love and light.

In this Earthwalk you will intentionally place yourself in a position that best allows you to connect with and collect Sun's nierika toward gaining energy and insight and healing power for any parts of your body that are injured. As you might suspect, the amount of energy received is directly proportionate to the level of connection attained. For this reason, you should be as free of negative emotions as possible and your strong intention must be evidenced by an open heart. The Earthwalks that have preceded this one will help you prepare to receive the healing and energizing gifts of Sun.

Begin this practice as the sun is rising. While you can perform this walk at any time and anywhere, it's best to be on easy, flat terrain in an area where you will be able to view the sunrise over the horizon.

Instructions for the Practice

1. Assume the Fox Stance with your arms comfortably at your sides, then raise your arms slightly and turn your hands so that your palms are facing forward and your fingers are extended and slightly separated. State your intention for the walk.

2. Take a few deep breaths and begin walking toward the sun as you see its first rays of light. Use your open hands to receive Sun's energy and then, if you wish, touch other parts of your body in order to give this energy directly to those places. Feel free to stop walking momentarily to do this, but continue moving as soon as you can. You can even increase the speed of your walk as the sun climbs higher and energizes you.

3. When Sun clears the horizon and enters the sky above, give him thanks for his energy, warmth, and light and say or even shout or sing anything else that comes from your heart—spontaneous words of love, problems in your life that you want to change, commitments for the future. Words from the heart that are spoken directly to the nierika of Sun are powerful medicine.

Comments on the Practice

If you do not have a place to perform this practice where you can view the sunrise while walking toward it, the next best thing is to walk in place. If that is not possible, you can perform this practice during another time of day, though morning is best. It is important not to stand still—you must walk and move to feel fully Sun's effects. If you arrive at the location of your walk early and have to wait for sunrise, it is best to face east and walk in place for a few minutes to help focus yourself for his arrival.

26. Sunset

Look at the colors in the sky at Sunset. The day that is fading away is like your inner being that is changing little by little, that has the freedom to transform, to grow . . . Look into those colors of the Sunset and see the being that you are, which is transforming.

MANOLO CETINA*

Sunset is a time of change and power—as the world converts from light to dark, the nierika changes and the shadows come together. The animals and beings animated during the hours of light become watchful, go to their dens, and prepare for the night while the creatures of the night begin to stir and the world for them begins to take shape and transform into familiar and welcome darkness.

This energy of change can be felt and used in a variety of ways. Just as sunset and sunrise can transform a day, you can transform your heart or an aspect of your life. And just as many colors fill the sky at sunset and sunrise, so too do many ways present themselves in which we can transform and change using our energy.

Begin this practice as the sun is setting. It's best to walk in an area from which you can view the sunset, but if that's not possible, at least walk in an area where you can see the colors of the sky changing during the sunset.

---

*Manolo Cetina, from a presentation in his workshop "The Spirit of the Earth," Michoacán, Mexico, 1996.

Instructions for the Practice

1. Begin in the Fox Stance and state out loud your intention for the walk.

2. As the sky starts to change colors, begin walking with your gaze fixed on the horizon. Notice how the sky transforms as day becomes night, how the light alters the colors that are part of this change.

3. Take note of your own state of transformation. See in the colors of the setting sun your own being and how you have changed and will continue to change throughout your life. Be aware that even in these few minutes of walking, you are transforming. Take this opportunity to see clearly the direction in which your life is moving, the shades and contrasts that color your life. Identify the small or big changes you wish to make, the alterations to your being that will allow you to fulfill your path in this magical life.

4. As the sun sets, say good-bye to those parts of yourself that you wish to change, or perhaps say farewell to someone in your past to whom you never had the courage to say good-bye, and, last of all, say goodnight to Sun, reminding him that you'll greet him the next morning when a new day and new beginning will come.

27. Illumination

We are luminous beings. Giving no importance to what our ego and our ideas tell us about ourselves, the essential truth about our nature remains in agreement with what our grandfathers expressed in ancient Tula: We are children of the Sun! Our nature is to Shine!

Victor Sanchez*

---

*Victor Sanchez, *Toltecs of the New Millennium* (Santa Fe: Bear & Company, 1996).

Sometimes due to the myriad activities revolving around our daily lives we forget that the energy and light of the sun truly live inside each one of us. Thoughts and concerns drive this knowledge into a place from which it can scarcely be found or remembered, but it is important that we regain this knowledge. Sun is not alone in his task of illuminating the world—because we have his energy and light within us, we have the ability to help him light the world.

Humans are capable of producing magnificent creations and spreading love and joy, but we also can be the most destructive and malevolent creatures on the planet. Connecting with Sun and helping him spread unconditional love, light, and energy—not making war and spreading hate and destruction—is the destiny of our species. War, hate, and destruction are all products of anthropocentrism, greed, and materialism. You must realize on a personal level—and accept as a personal responsibility—your destiny as a little Sun. In doing so you will affect all those around you. This is the central theme of this Earthwalk—taking the love and light that you find through living this joyous gift of life and spreading it to others just as Sun spreads his light and energy, learning how to duplicate those unique moments when you dropped the trivialities and concerns of the daily world and became a little Sun upon Earth.

This Earthwalk has two parts: The first part involves collecting or refreshing your light and the second part focuses on spreading it.

Instructions for the Practice

1. Begin with a recapitulation of some special moments in your life. To do this, start Walk 1, Walk of Attention, and call to mind a moment from your life that was filled with love and light. Try to feel or relive that moment all over again. Travel deep into the memory and try to keep this feeling with you as you walk. When you feel ready, find another moment to recapitulate, and another after that—perhaps a kiss shared with someone you love, a hike to a beautiful place, the moment of

attaining a long-worked-for goal. As you walk, let the memory of these moments fill your body with light, each one making you shine brighter from within.

2. When you sense this light within, be sure you are facing Sun as you move—feel his warmth and energy entering your body, his unconditional love and nierika, then take that nierika and join it with the light emanating from your body full of memories so that you are all light, inside and out. You are now walking as a little Sun upon Earth. The same attributes of Father Sun emanate from you. Hold onto this feeling as you continue.

3. The second part of the practice begins as you leave your walking place and return to your everyday world filled with human interactions. Now comes the time when you fulfill your destiny and share with those around you the light and energy you have received. Remember that the goal is not to judge or change anyone, but rather to radiate your light so that others may absorb it. Even if you say nothing to those around you, you can send your good intentions and love directly to them—simply feel the light moving from you to them unconditionally and silently. Return to this walk often—perhaps each day—to transform yourself and others.

Comments on the Practice

Collecting the Sun nierika in this walk, as in Walk 25, Sunrise, is something completely natural to all of Earth's beings. Every moment of every day plants are collecting sun and transforming it into the sugars that feed the world and the oxygen that gives us breath. This same nierika also touches the world and our eyes so that we can see, and gives warmth to our skin. The nierika that lives in the sun certainly lives within us as well—so to spread light is as natural as receiving it. As biochemist and Nobel laureate Albert Szent-Györgyi wrote, "What drives life is thus a little electric current, set up by the sunshine."

Remember that it's not necessary to verbally spread your light. Offering a nice word or kind remark may be perfectly suitable for a given moment, but it's just as effective to spread light behind the scenes. Doing so will allow you to shine without calling attention to your actions—just as the nierika of Sun does each day.

WATER

When the water breaks, we are born into a world of living systems that are nourished and maintained by this sacred fluid. Like the veins in our body, rivers run through Mother Earth, and as she rotates, her oceans interact with the moon, sun, and cosmos.

We live in an atmosphere of rain, snow, wind, clouds, and humidity—all of which connect us to the water that graces us with life. With every breath and every bead of sweat we expend her, and then replenish ourselves through the food and drink she provides. Water is the sacred spring that is our source.

The water in our world not only sustains life but is also a profound source of inspiration and beauty and as such holds many lessons for us. By watching, listening to, and feeling the many different expressions of the nierika of Water, we can learn much about ourselves and our world.

Water can take many forms and can change shape depending on the circumstance and surroundings. She can rush into a drinking glass we fill, she can flow in the form of a stream or a river, she can rise in great waves in the ocean or lie as quiet as glass in the form of a pond or puddle. She moves with grace, fluidity, and incredible power—of this we should take note. But Water can also teach us how to be still, and how to reflect like a mirror the world around us.

We can bring the lessons of this nierika into our daily lives, enriching our experience and connecting ourselves in one more way with the power of the natural world.

28. Fluidity

The nierika of Water expresses fluidity as it runs through the riverbeds flowing around and over obstacles, by the endless chant of the river and the incessant waves of the Sea. In the case of human beings, fluidity expresses as the possibility of facing in an efficient way, the complex situations that life puts in front of us. In order to act with fluidity in our everyday life, it is necessary that our ego loosens its rigidity so that we are able to use all of our resources.

MANOLO CETINA*

This Earthwalk leads you to move with Water's physical fluidity, but also with an internal fluidity of attitude and feeling inspired by her. By emulating the flowing nature of Water, we come upon much less resistance as we travel through life. Making our path one of least resistance does not imply timidity or a propensity for avoiding work or obstacles. On the contrary, it suggests that, like water, we are able to flow on our appointed path—which may mean over, under, around, or through the many obstacles that cross it.

Instructions for the Practice

1. To begin this practice, find a place where you can walk next to a river, stream, or lake. The size of the water is not as important as its flow—water that is flowing is best.

2. Locate yourself close to the water (at a safe distance, if it is dangerously deep or fast-moving) and close your eyes. Listen for a few minutes to the endless chant of Water, singing the song of fluidity that is unique to that particular place.

3. Open your eyes and watch Water flowing and expressing her

---

*Manolo Cetina, from a presentation in his workshop "The Jump to the Other Self," Ajusco, Mexico, 1997.

fluidity. Let your thoughts, feelings, and perceptions rise to the surface and be carried away with the current. At the same time, feel the magic of Water flowing through your veins in the form of your lifeblood—you and Water are the same.

4. Stay with this feeling for a few minutes and then begin to walk in a way that carries the fluidity of Water with you. At the same moment you begin to walk, repeat the word *fluidity* to yourself as you use your body to express the feeling of the word as it lives inside you. Your steps are sure but light as you float over and around obstacles in your path. Listen to the music of Water as her flowing caresses your soul. You and she are one; you have joined with the nierika of Water, you express it in your motion.

5. Thoroughly explore your transformation for at least twenty minutes and then stop walking and stand close to the water again. This time, as you look into the Water nierika, see your life. See how you react when faced with obstacles, with fears, with your unfulfilled dreams. Take a few minutes and, in a detached manner, watch the events of your life as they are shown to you and be sure to notice how you have dealt with them.

6. Next, looking into the flowing Water, see yourself facing your obstacles with fluidity. Feel her giving you strength—use it to help you dream a more fluid way to handle these situations in your life. Watch yourself accomplishing your goals and facing your fears with grace and power.

7. Make a commitment to your desire to be a more fluid being: Call to mind a specific task that you can readily accomplish. State your commitment to Water out loud.

8. Last, give thanks to Water and, as you leave the area to walk back into your life, carry her gift of fluidity. Accomplish your commitment as a concrete act of connection to her.

Comments on the Practice

This walk can be used whenever you visit flowing water. Even though they are all connected through the cycles of tides and rain, each flowing river or stream and each body of water has specific and unique qualities to offer. Each has the power to share insights, knowledge, and her own unique songs.

When using this technique, be sure to listen with all your heart and being—Water's message may come as a song with words or in a way that is completely new to you. On a cautionary note, please be careful when working with a large body of water—the strength of the nierika of Water can be overpowering, especially when your energy or mood is low. For the first few times, it is usually best to open up to her when she is in a very safe and peaceful form such as a natural spring or small brook or river. These places usually have an energy that is happy and light, unlike the ocean, which can be extremely powerful and somber.

An important technique for connecting with the flowing rivers of your body is to become conscious of your heartbeat—to actually feel the pumping of your heart as it sends your blood (which is 90 percent water) through your veins and arteries. While listening to the beat of your heart is a wonderful way to become deeply centered and still, it also works to help you develop fluidity in your thoughts and motion.

29. Still Motion

As you watched, a great stillness came into you. The brain itself became very quiet, without any reaction, without a movement, and it was strange to feel this immense stillness. "Feel" isn't the word. The quality of that silence, that stillness, is not felt by the brain; it is beyond the brain. . . . You are so still that your body becomes completely part of Earth, part of everything that is still. And as the slight breeze came

from the hills, stirring the leaves, this stillness, this
extraordinary quality of silence, was not disturbed.

J. KRISHNAMURTI*

This Earthwalk will help you to understand Water's lesson that all things are connected and will help make you aware of how you can retain stillness in the midst of motion.

Instructions for the Practice

1. Begin your walk in an area near a calm lake or pond.

2. Stand by the water and notice its stillness—especially that it can appear still even when it is in motion. This same skill is valuable to humans as well—we can learn to be still even while we are moving through our lives. As you stand quietly next to the water, try to internalize this feeling of moving stillness.

3. Begin walking in a way that expresses this feeling. Don't worry about the physical aspect of your movement; focus instead on what is happening inside. Simply walk in a way that calms you. Feel your heart slowing and, as you walk, your mind growing still. If you need help acquiring or maintaining stillness, look at the water and draw in the Water nierika. Walk with this feeling of moving stillness for at least twenty minutes, then stop walking and stand facing the water again.

4. This time concentrate on seeing the reflections in the calm water. Notice for a few minutes how the water can act like a mirror that reflects whatever is around it.

5. Next look into that mirror and see your life—how you yourself reflect your life circumstances and interactions whether they are good or bad. See yourself when you are judging other people: Are you simply casting onto them your own image of what's

---

*J. Krishnamurti, *Meditations* (Boston: Shambhala, 1979).

right? See yourself when you blame someone: Are you perhaps displacing the blame from yourself? See how you reflect joy during the happy moments of your life. See through the magic mirror of nierika how you reflect other people's thoughts, moods, and feelings, and how you reflect the people and institutions that shape our world. Don't rush this step; take your time.

6. Now pick up a small stone from the ground nearby. Moving close to the still water, drop it in and notice that this affects not only the immediate area where the stone entered the water but, as evidenced by the ripples that spread farther and farther out from this point, reaches a surprisingly vast portion of the pond or lake as well. Ultimately, because the water is one fluid, connected body, the whole of it is affected by your one simple action.

7. Begin walking slowly again and feel with each step how we are all connected in the same way—every one of our actions, no matter how small, ultimately affects everything around us. As you walk, realize that your life is like the calm water and your actions and those of others function just like the stone you dropped.

8. As your walk comes to an end and you return to your daily life, keep with you these lessons of Water and call them forward prior to each of your actions.

Comments on the Practice

The magical quality of water in still motion—reflecting the world while fluidly moving into ever-changing forms—can be found inside us as well. When we see our reflection in a mirror, we usually perceive ourselves as a solid body that is slowly changing as we grow older. But in reality, more than half the weight of our body is water—in fact, our brain is more than 75 percent water—and as this water flows through us, our body is constantly renewing itself. Water is the fundamental building component of all life. But it doesn't end there—we now know that there is water on the moon, in the sun, and even in the so-called empty spaces among the stars. Beyond showing us that everything in our world is connected, water is one of our primary connections to the universe.

30. Rain

Without the Rains we have nothing. When they do not come
we look for the reason in our actions. What have we done
so that we have lost this blessing?

TAYAU (ALFREDO GONZALES PONCIANO)*

Who among us hasn't felt the blessing of the rain as it falls from the heavens to grace Earth with life-giving moisture? The cycles of growth and decay that sustain our world are directly linked to the gift of rain. For this reason it has been worshiped and praised throughout human history, thanked when it is abundant, and pleaded with and prayed to when it is scarce. Hundreds of gods and goddesses from numerous religions, cultures, and pagan sects have been named in its honor and countless ceremonies have and still do exist for calling it forth and honoring it.

Modern people often view the rain quite differently from how our ancestors did, reducing this great and necessary gift to merely another piece of the weather forecast in the daily news. It is not hard to see how this came to be—people in developed countries are so far removed from the sources of their water and food that they have come to take them for granted. Indeed, many people today would be hard-pressed to say where their tap water actually comes from or how it is collected, maintained, and distributed.

But in truth we are in danger of losing forever our supplies of fresh water. The rate at which we pollute and manipulate this

---

*Tayau (Alfredo Gonzales Ponciano), Huichol president of the Union of Jicareros of Jalisco, keepers of the sacred Huichol traditions, personal conversation in the Huichol Sierra, 1998.

sacred gift to feed our materialism is nothing less than astounding. And the rain is certainly not immune to this degradation. In many parts of the world it has become poison to the living beings that it once nourished. This tragedy can be corrected only by realizing our reciprocal relationship to the water that sustains our world.

The intention of this walk is to joyfully rediscover the magic of rain as it falls from the sky and into our lives, to rekindle a child-like love of dancing in the rain while at the same time realizing the profound importance that it plays in our lives.

Of course, this walk requires that it be raining. A gentle, steady rain that is not too strong and temperature conditions that are comfortable are the ideal, but don't wait for these perfect conditions. More important is getting out into the world and experiencing this blessing without delay. Try to walk in a place where Nature, not concrete, reigns. Performing this practice free of clothing will add to the experience but is not mandatory. It's best not to completely alienate yourself from the rain, however, by wearing a full rain suit. The object of the walk is to allow you to connect with the rain as viscerally as possible—even a hat and umbrella can interfere with this.

Instructions for the Practice

1. Begin by standing in the rain with your eyes closed. Feel the water falling on your body and running down your face, arms, torso, and legs. Take deep breaths and smell the rain and all the scents that it brings out in your surroundings. Hear the rain as it lands—see if you can pick out the specific sounds of the drops falling on rocks, ground, and plants around you. Listen to, feel, and breathe in the rain for a few minutes.

2. Next, open your eyes and begin to walk. Notice all the living beings that drink the rain to sustain their lives and single out each one that you see or hear as you walk. After a time, begin to

attend to the cycle of life and death that surrounds you and how the falling rain plays a major part in this.

3. Stop walking, close your eyes, and simply stand still. Imagine yourself as a tree or other being in your surroundings and receive the rain as this being would. Feel the rain's nourishment filling your whole body. Now imagine what would happen to you if you never had another drink of this liquid. Raise your arms to the sky and thank the Water nierika for the blessed gift of rain that nourishes us.

4. Give yourself fully to the feelings you have for the rain at this time. Let yourself dance, cry, sing, laugh, stamp your feet. Let your feelings pour out just as the rain pours from the clouds and allow yourself to be carried away just as the raindrops merging with the water in a river are carried away.

5. Finally, before returning home make a commitment to honor our reciprocal relationship with Water and carry this pledge into your daily life.

Comments on the Practice

Water not only was necessary for the evolution of our species; it also is necessary for its survival. Although our salty sweat and tears remind us of our ocean origins, we, like so many other beings, cannot live on salt water. We depend entirely on the hydrologic cycle of rain in which the energy from the sun causes water from the oceans to evaporate and rise into the atmosphere, after which this water vapor condenses and falls back to Earth as rain, which seeps into the ground and replenishes the rivers so that the cycle can repeat itself. Because we survive by taking in water and the life-forms that are grown and sustained by it, the water within us is connected in the most sacred way possible to the water outside of us. Care for the water outside of us translates into care for the water within us.

This can lead to some possible commitments to make at the end of your walk: Perhaps you could make a commitment to conserve water throughout your daily routine, or to avoid the purchase of products sold by companies that divert or destroy natural water supplies, or to develop a sacred relationship with all the water in your life by respecting it and consciously acknowledging how you use it and why.

There are many ways we can improve our use of water in our lives, and we should begin right now. It is true that absence makes the heart grow fonder ... but in the case of water, absence means death.

MOTHER EARTH

Earth is a living being. She is our mother, our provider, and our protector, an ancient being whose life blesses us in countless ways and whose inexhaustible and unconditional love is expressed day after day through giving us all we have while expecting nothing in return. She feeds us, gives us a home, provides us with beauty and mystery, and sustains us and all of our brothers and sisters who share this life with us.

Connecting with Mother Earth requires the awareness of her as a living and breathing being. Such awareness opens your heart to her enormous presence, allowing you to receive the warmth and unconditional love that she offers us every moment of our lives. Such awareness has the power to cure illnesses of the heart, vanquish loneliness, and restore hope and joy to your life.

The belief of human beings around the world that we can own pieces of Earth allows so many to ignore their obligation to care for her in the name of all of us. All of us, after all, interact in a matrix of sacred energy that has Earth at its center.

There has never been a more important task for humanity than to wake up to the folly of our attitudes toward Earth and accept our appointed role: As children of Earth and Sun it is our duty and privilege to care for our parents, to learn about the currents and cycles of life, and to develop an understanding of how we can not only fit into Earth's tapestry in a harmonious way, but also contribute to it with positive energy and a sustainable way of life. Surely Mother Earth and Father Sun are looking at us right now and wondering when we will begin walking this wise and healthy path.

This book does not pretend to hold any specific answers to the complex problems humanity faces concerning the development of sustainable ways of life. But the formulation of problem-solving skills to address these difficulties must be born from pure love or else we will continue to argue about the solutions. Even people who seemingly have the same good intentions of realizing their roles as caretakers of Earth still fight and bicker among themselves because they are not able to put their controlling egos aside and just listen to Earth for guidance. This is what the Earthwalks described in this book help us do. If they can guide one person to truly lay aside self-importance and realize through the pure love of Earth his or her role on the planet as a child of Earth and Sun, then they will have accomplished their task.

31. Love Healing

Earth is our Mother. From her we receive the nourishment for our body and the energy that strengthens us and gives us life. We are never alone; Earth accompanies and sustains us in all moments of life. . . . She is that enormous being whose inexhaustible love aids in curing afflictions and sadness, who washes away pettiness and yields power and secrets when we put forgetfulness and personal history aside and humbly open our spirit to her sweet presence.

MANOLO CETINA*

Nature is the visible body of Mother Earth—to know her is to love her and to know how to show her our love. There is no better way to show our appreciation than simply to spend time with her. That is the focus of this Earthwalk.

We also receive benefits from giving our time to Earth. In the presence of Nature's majesty our personal problems are placed in their proper perspective. Speaking your concerns to the rocks of a mountain or the sands of a desert can relieve their weight even to

---

*Manolo Cetina, from a presentation at the workshop "Burial of the Warrior," Toronto, Ontario, Canada, 1998.

the point that you may begin to laugh at yourself. This is very good medicine and although it won't make the problems go away, it will give you renewed power over them.

Instructions for the Practice

1. Perform this walk anywhere you choose as long as you have Earth beneath your feet. For the first time, try to pick a location that is an especially impressive expression of her beauty. If your place is safe for barefoot walking, consider this as a way of growing even closer to her. Before starting, state your intention to her: Telling her that you are glad to be with her again, state that you wish to be healed of your wounds.

2. As you begin to walk, try to feel Earth's enormous energy beneath your feet. Breathe deeply and begin telling her the problems and challenges you are facing in your life. Talk to her as if she were your best friend—don't hold back. She doesn't judge you for your mistakes and she won't punish you.

3. When you have finished talking, you are ready to fully receive Earth's energy. This is accomplished through both your breathing and her energy itself. Continue walking and as you do, draw in Earth's energy with your breath: Inhale through your nose very deeply and strongly, then exhale slowly and shallowly. In this process the inhalation portion of the complete breath becomes dominant. As you breathe, feel the energy of Earth entering through the soles of your feet. Slowly it will fill your legs, your genitals, your torso, arms, neck, head, and finally your mind. By this time her energy is glowing from within you.

4. At the moment when you feel you are full and that the energy has reached the top of your head, be aware that the remaining thoughts and emotions keeping you from realizing your dreams are being pushed out of your being through the top of your

head. Now the energy of Earth can flow through you unimpeded, connecting you to all that surrounds you. Like a great tree that takes nourishment from Earth and gives off oxygen, you are a conduit receiving energy from Earth and spreading love to the heavens. At this time you might shout with joy or scream or cry or dance. Thank the nierika of Earth for absorbing your impediments and, by doing so, creating room for her life-giving force.

Comments on the Practice

The indigenous people I walk with often use this technique of drawing up the energy of Earth, especially on long trips during which they actually seem to get stronger the more they walk! Use this form of walking whenever you feel you need to release and replenish, or when you are feeling lonely or down. Mother Earth will always accept and help you.

32. Cycles

*At first we all think we can outrun the death aspect of the Life/
Death/Life nature. The fact is we cannot. It follows right along
behind us, bumpety-bump, thumpety-thump, right into our houses,
right into our consciousness. . . . In feminine imagery, the Death
Woman, Death Mother, or Death Maiden always was understood
as the carrier of destiny, the maker, the harvest maiden, the mother,
the river-walker, and the re-creator; all of these in cycle.*

CLARISSA PINKOLA ESTES*

This Earthwalk has two main components: The first deals with the awareness of death and the second with energetic rebirth. Reaching an awareness of death should not be viewed as a morbid or scary process. Accepting with a healthy perspective the one

---

*Clarissa Pinkola Estes, *Women Who Run with the Wolves* (New York: Ballantine Books, 1992).

inevitable circumstance of life can actually give power and force of intention to your actions. If you knew that tomorrow wouldn't come, what would you do today? We are all guilty of putting off for a possibly nonexistent tomorrow sharing those things that we may share right now. Because of this, keeping the awareness of our mortality with us can ultimately be empowering. At the same time, however, it is important to remember as we act today that even if we ourselves may not have a tomorrow, our children and grand-children still have theirs. For this reason we must live our lives fully today but temper our actions in the interest of future genera-tions. This allows us the force of intention to live fulfilling lives while, at the same time, maintaining balance to ensure that those beyond us may live tomorrow.

Quite often a near-death experience heightens this awareness of mortality—but this walk allows you to powerfully and effec-tively cultivate this awareness without such a drastic circumstance through drawing upon the energy of Earth and asking for her support and help. Through the energy of her unconditional love you will be able to safely explore the awareness of death in a way that provides meaning and purpose.

The second main component of this walk consists of refilling your being with the energy of Earth in order to replenish those parts of you that have "died." This energy is free from the taint of unhealthy habits and destructive ways, and through its cleanliness and purity you are given a fresh energetic configuration with which to interact with the world.

First select a place for your walk. While this will depend on availability and your personal physical condition, the optimum set-ting is one that will enable you to walk for approximately one hour, at the end of which you will be close to your physical limit. This means that if you are a person in excellent condition who is accus-tomed to running in marathons, you should find yourself a steep mountain trail and proceed at full speed. Conversely, if you are in poor shape or have specific physical limitations, you may choose a flat area and move at a slower pace that is nevertheless challenging for you to sustain for an hour. The goal is to reach your maximum exertion level without being dead tired after an hour of walking.

One last suggestion is that you find a place that is private where you will not be disturbed or inhibited by other people.

Instructions for the Practice

1. Assume the Fox Stance, state out loud your intention for the walk, and begin Walk 1, the Walk of Attention.

2. After your thoughts have become quiet and you have walked for a few minutes, begin to spontaneously recapitulate specific moments of your life from childhood to the present. In this form of recapitulation, you simply call to your mind's eye an event from your life, explore the feelings of that moment, and briefly try to relive the experience for a few minutes while walking. Over the span of about one hour, begin with moments from your childhood and work forward chronologically until you reach the significant moments of your present life.

3. When your recapitualtion of events takes you to those that happened recently, increase your level of physical exertion so that when you reach the event nearest to the present you are close to your physical limit. When your body feels ready, fall gently to the ground, being very careful not to hurt yourself. This moment represents the instant just before your death.

4. While lying on the ground facedown, firmly plant your hands on the earth and close your eyes. Try to evoke the feeling that these are your last moments on the planet. Start by saying good-bye to your loved ones, one at a time, in a loud voice. Do it with emotion strong enough that they might actually feel it. Next, say good-bye to all the beautiful things you have seen and felt in this life—the birds, the trees, the sunsets, making love, feeling

the heat of a warm fire, and so forth. Finally, ask for forgiveness from the people you have hurt and forgive the people who have hurt you. Do all of this out loud as if this were your very last opportunity to speak these things. This should take between five and ten minutes.

5. Now, without planning or thinking, spontaneously speak your last words in this life. Don't make a speech—you haven't the time because death is about to touch you. After your last words, stop talking, let your body go limp, and let all thoughts leave your mind. This moment represents your death.

6. For the next few minutes be aware of the ground and the air around you and slowly begin to imagine that you are decomposing, that time is moving forward and water and wind are turning your body into dust and carrying you away.

   Now imagine that your awareness is above the ground, looking down, but you are not there; your body has been returned to Earth. Stay with this feeling for a few minutes and then slowly move so that you are kneeling on the ground with your eyes closed and your hands still firmly on the earth.

7. Return your awareness to your body and realize that death has passed you by this time. You are alive! Breathe deeply and thank Mother Earth for the gift of life. Feel her energy fill the vessel of your body with power and love.

8. Stand up, slowly open your eyes, and see with renewed sight the beauty around you—draw into yourself through your eyes all the surrounding manifestations of Earth's love. Realize in this moment not only that you are the same as all the beings that surround you, but also that as a human being you are a caretaker whose sacred responsibility it is to watch over your mother.

9. Begin to walk again as you see through the eyes of Nature what you will do with this second chance at life. Now is the time for your dreams and for a life lived in harmony with Earth.

10. Make decisions and commitments for this new life and walk back into the world carrying your newfound energy and power.

Comments on the Practice

This walk should be physically challenging, but to ensure your safety, do not exceed your limit. Remember, too, that focusing on the internal aspects of the walk will require considerable energy.

Be aware that your experience with this practice may indeed be life altering. Allowing yourself to fully explore the feeling of not being alive anymore can enable you to cut through the trivialities of your daily existence and see clearly what means the most to you in this life. Don't be afraid to find out. Our existence passes in the blink of an eye, and there is no better time than right now to enter into the life that you "know" you want to live and to make real those actions that will take you there. Earth can help guide you and give you strength.

33. Developing Reciprocity

Now is the time to share with all life on our maltreated planet Earth by deepening our identification with all life forms, with ecosystems, and with Gaia, this fabulous Old planet of ours . . . We can all contribute to this individually, and it is also a question of politics, local and global. Part of the joy stems from the consciousness of our own intimate relation to something bigger than our own ego, something which has endured for millions of years and is worth continued life for millions of years. The requisite care flows naturally if the self is widened and deepened so that protection of free nature is felt and conceived of as protection of our very selves.

ARNE NAESS*

---

*Arne Naess, "Self-Realization," in *Thinking Like a Mountain: Towards a Council of All Beings* (New Society Publishers, 1988).

There are many ways in which you can fulfill your sacred inheritance as a caretaker of Earth, but having completed your brush with death and its subsequent energetic infusion in Walk 32, Cycles, one way is to begin an intentional reciprocal relationship with Earth on the level of energy and love. This may seem to be an impractical approach as compared to developing green power alternatives, lobbying against irresponsible logging, or starting a more aggressive recycling program in your home—but in fact these kinds of activities will be given more force if you empower yourself through intentional energetic reciprocity with Earth.

What does this mean? First, it involves fully realizing the gifts bestowed on us by our mother, and second, it means reciprocating by giving back to her unconditional love and energy. This takes time, but there is no better moment to start than this one—after taking far too long, the sooner we begin giving, the sooner we can restore balance.

This Earthwalk helps you develop a strong energetic connection to a specific place in Nature that will become for you a personal place of power where you can give to and receive energy from Earth. Your walk to this place is your sacred pilgrimage to the home of your mother, a journey that not only leads to a relationship, but results in your taking care of this place on a physical, energetic, and spiritual level as well.

Since everything on Mother Earth is connected, you may wonder why it's necessary to choose a place—why can't we simply use whatever place we happen to be in at the moment? The answer has more to do with practicality than with function. True, if we nourish one place on Earth the whole Earth will receive it, but the fact is that most of us are real beginners in this process and as such it's much easier to find a place that has naturally drawn us and learn to develop our relationship there. From there we can use our increased energy and awareness to connect in a meaningful way with other places or even many places at once. Making pilgrimages to different places of power is an exciting and beneficial way to connect and learn from Earth, but will ultimately be most effective if we first develop a deep and meaningful connection to one specific, chosen place.

Instructions for the Practice

1. Select your place in a practical but meaningful manner. If you have progressed through all of the walks in this book up to this point, then you have already started to develop relationships with certain areas of Nature. You could choose one of these places, or a place where you had a special experience or gained some insight. Remember that since your relationship is going to be developed over a period of time and through many occasions, you will want a place that is readily accessible to you, is part of the natural world, and is private enough for you to be alone there for periods of time. If this is not possible, then use your internal resources and ask Mother Earth to help you. The only places you should steer away from are those that are physically dangerous or are already places of power (such as archaeological sites, ruins, and active places of worship).

2. Once you have chosen your place in Nature, you must next define its boundaries by following your heart and asking Mother Earth to help you because, after all, it is her house you will be visiting. Remember that the bigger the house, the more energy it will take to keep it up, so don't go overboard. A nice "starter house" might consist of from ten to twenty square yards. Walk the boundaries of your area and place a rock or small object in each corner or in a few places around the perimeter, if you like.

3. Next, begin constructing the foundation of this house. Choose and mark a location for a front door through which you will enter and exit with full attention and intention every time you visit. In traditions that use circles for activities similar to this

walk, the door is placed in the east in reverence to the rising sun.

4. Upon entering the house, begin walking slowly in a clockwise direction around the perimeter of the house until you have completed five full trips. Each time you pass the front door, honor one of the five main nierikas (Earth, Fire, Sun, Water, and Wind) by recalling a specific event during which he or she touched your life. For example, you may honor the Water nierika by recalling the joyous feeling of rain falling on your face, or Earth by recalling a particularly beautiful flower or tree.

5. After completing these five walks, reverse your direction and walk another series of five trips around the perimeter, this time bringing to mind a manifestation of Earth's gifts each time you pass the front door. For example the first time around you may recall the food that you most love, the second time around you recall the feeling of warm sand between your toes, the third time around, the smell of wildflowers, and so on. Walk slowly and deliberately and be aware that recapitulating such remembrances moves energy on both a physical level (through the movement of your body) and a spiritual level (through honoring the nierikas, thereby establishing a connection with the life force that animates everything).

6. When you have completed your ten walks around the perimeter, move to the center of the house and plant your hands on the ground. State out loud your intention to develop a meaningful relationship with her and to construct a house for her that represents unconditional love and concrete offerings in the form of words from your heart and actions to nurture and protect her.

7. Now comes the moment in which you open your heart and share your energy with Earth. The level of honesty with which you do so will determine the strength of the foundation of your house. This is your chance to enable massive amounts of energy to move within yourself. Tell Mother Earth about your

feelings, your life, your failures and victories, your problems and wishes. Don't hold back and don't feel self-conscious. Words from the heart are powerful and by sharing them you will be establishing a connection with Earth that runs far deeper than the meaning of the actual words.

8. Once you have finished with this initial exchange of energy, express your thanks and make a commitment to continue developing your relationship with her. Be sure to walk out through the front door to reenter your life.

Comments on the Practice

You can continue to build your house through sharing words from your heart; keeping your place as pristine as you found it (or more so, if it had already been touched by humans in a destructive way); and making offerings (see part 5, Offering and Vision), which will keep your relationship in a state of growth and strength. The first offering should be to continue to visit your house during each season of the year—as seasons pass, your house will undergo drastic transformations and by visiting often you will deepen your connection to the cycles and currents of life. Through walking to and exploring your house you will be exploring yourself and developing an outlet for living in a chaotic world. Be sure to tell Earth about your actions to protect and honor her, about your challenges and frustrations, and bring her gifts to express your love.

Once your connection to your place is established and you are completely comfortable and at ease when visiting, you will be able to ask and receive answers to specific questions—however, bear in mind that answers may be revealed in unexpected ways. They may arrive in forms as equally powerful and magical as Earth herself.

It is interesting to note that while indigenous cultures have inhabited the same areas for sometimes hundreds of generations, our modern lives have made us much more transient. For instance, most of the inhabitants of the United States have come from families that have immigrated here either by force or choice as far back as three hundred years ago or as recently as yesterday. Our lifestyles also encourage transience—we change jobs, relocate, travel. All of this transience amounts to yet another reason that so many people do not feel a deep connection to the land. This can be changed, however, by each of us intentionally connecting.

This Earthwalk can be the beginning of your Earth-honoring tradition, your means of establishing this connection, and each visit to this house can become a pilgrimage made to honor Earth's power and grace.

34. Heartbeat

*So the singing of song and using the heart as drum are both
mystical acts awakening layers of the psyche not much used or
seen. The breath or pneuma flowing over us shakes open certain
apertures, rouses certain otherwise inaccessible faculties. We
cannot say for each person what will be sung up, drummed up,
because these open such odd and unusual apertures
in the human who participates thusly.*

Clarissa Pinkola Estes*

The heartbeat of Earth is expressed by the rhythms of Nature, which play in us as well. For this Earthwalk you will use a drum as a vehicle to help you connect with Earth's heartbeat. The drum is an ancient instrument and tool that can itself impart great knowledge and light. If you don't already own one, you can borrow or purchase one for this practice, though the best drum for this walk and for connection to the nierikas in general is one that you make yourself from natural materials. In any case, your drum ideally should be one that is made by someone who has developed a

---

*Clarissa Pinkola Estes, *Women Who Run with the Wolves* (New York: Ballantine Books, 1992).

spiritual connection to Earth. Remember that as you proceed on your own journey of connection, your intention and the elements that nurture it will gain power, leading companions and tools like drums to come to you when you need and often least expect them.

Instructions for the Practice

1. Arrive at your walking place with your drum and state your intention out loud.

2. Assume the Fox Stance and begin to walk, silently carrying your drum with you as you establish a rhythm between your walk and your breath.

3. Once this rhythm is clear, establish a rhythm with your surroundings, which will manifest internally and be related to what is happening in the natural world around you. The rhythm of spring, for example, is quick and varied as the plants blossom and the animals birth and feed and grow. The rhythm of winter is still and quiet. The rhythm of sunrise is a busy, pulsing hum, while that of the afternoon is a slow, lazy, steady beating. Remember that all of Nature's rhythms are constantly flowing and changing, however subtly, which means you will need to tap into what is happening in the specific moment and place of your walk rather than making assumptions based on previous experience. This is best done by paying close attention to the activities of the animals and plants around you. Walk for a few moments to establish this internal rhythm.

4. Next, begin drumming by finding two different tones on the face of the drum that you can play one after the other, matching each tone to each step of your walk in a repeating left step/ tone A, right step/tone B pattern. Beating the center of the drum will produce different tones from tapping the edge.

5. After accomplishing this, match your drumming/walking beat

to the rhythm of Nature around you, which is now your internal rhythm. As you walk, explore the specific feelings and rhythms of the areas you pass through. Sometimes they will be fast, sometimes slow; sometimes you will hear them soft, sometimes loud. Be aware of the level of energy around you and its fluctuations and adjust yourself both internally and physically, using the beat of the drum and the movement of your body. For example, if a huge jet comes flying overhead obliterating all other sounds, the energy of the beings around you will certainly be affected (perhaps, as is common in such circumstances, it will manifest as a feeling of suspended breath).

6. Give yourself the opportunity to explore this walk for extended periods of time until you are able, eventually, to merge your heartbeat with the natural world. Experiencing this rhythmic connection with Earth will bring renewed strength and joy to your life.

Comments on the Practice

Much like picking up a musical instrument for the first time or playing with a new band, it can take a little time to coordinate with the rhythm of Nature. While there aren't any rules for accomplishing this, one suggestion is to match your rhythm with that of your surroundings, but also to allow yourself to play an occasional solo. For example, if on a bright and sunny day a cloud momentarily covers the sun, you could slow your walk and drumbeat even if there are no perceptible changes around you.

FIRE

Fire is the father of Sun and is therefore called Grandfather Fire. His energy fills the universe and lives inside everything. It is no small wonder that people love to sit around the campfire or have fireplaces in their homes that really aren't used for heat. We are all easily mesmerized by the dancing energy of the flames, but there is much more to Grandfather Fire than most people realize, and to really know him is to experience a profound source of enlightened energy.

Fire is a great teacher and source of knowledge and is used by the most powerful shamans of the world to guide the lives of their communities and to connect directly with spirit and power. There is so much to know about the nierika of Fire that you could make it a lifelong study and still only touch upon its great mystery.

35. Connect to the Universe

I keep the life of the Fire in the flame of my candle, and I take care of the flame. I spend the whole night taking care of it, because in this way I am taking care of every single being in the world. The fire gives you the life, the fire is in my heart, and I have learned to take care of him. With him I can walk through the darkness of the world and I have always a light, lighting my path.

MARAKAME TONIO CUCHURI*

The intention of this Earthwalk is to see that Fire within us is the same as the Fire nierika, and to understand that it is through this energy that we connect to the universe.

---

*Marakame Tonio Cuchuri, Huichol healer and shaman who sings the voice of the Fire, personal conversation during a pilgrimage, Mexico, 1999.

Prepare to perform this walk outdoors at night when it is easier to see and feel Fire. Bring with you a candle and, if there is any wind, a safe container to keep the flame from being blown out.

Instructions for the Practice

1. Arrive where you will be walking and light your candle.

2. Begin to walk, holding your candle in one hand in front of you at about chest level and keeping your free hand in front of the flame. Remember that because you are walking in the dark, you should be extra aware of your surroundings and should use care and caution as you step. As much as you can, try to use the night vision you developed in Walk 9, Night Vision. Focus your attention between the light of the candle and the darkness surrounding it and develop your awareness of how the light of the flame contrasts with that darkness.

3. After a few minutes have passed, stop walking and look directly at the flame, focusing your vision and attention on it completely. Watch how it dances and flickers. Notice the variety of soft hues in the flame and how the tip of it is in constant motion. Let its flowing expression of energy and nierika flood your awareness to such an extent that everything else falls away. Take as long as you need to with this step.

4. Next, lift your eyes from the flame, begin walking again, and softly focus on the world around you while maintaining your awareness of the flame as a flowing and luminous expression of energy in the middle of the darkness. This light is an expression of the light of knowledge that the nierika of Fire can bring to your life. He is your beacon in the night of mystery that surrounds us, the light that guides you. Feel the moving energy of the flame as you walk slowly, and make your step an expression of this movement: Try to walk like a moving flame of energy by internalizing the flowing transfer of energy from the

candle to the atmosphere. Continue walking in this manner until you feel compelled to stop and look only at the flame again.

5. Focus your attention on the flame, watching the tip of it with all your being and the intention of discovering how it gives off its light and energy in an upward release. See and feel how this brilliant energy feeds and joins with the energy moving all around us and throughout the universe.

6. Now close your eyes and "see" the flame of Fire inside your heart. Fire lives inside each of us. Hold this vision for a few minutes and then open your eyes and try to see the living flame of the candle and Fire in your heart at the same time. Grandfather Fire lives in you—carry this knowledge with you and you will never be alone.

7. Now put out the flame and begin to walk again, noticing how the absence of the light of the flame causes you to feel. As you walk in the dark, remember how different it was walking with Fire. This is how it feels to be unaware that Fire lives within you.

Comments on the Practice

From this Earthwalk you can develop a relationship with Grandfather Fire by speaking your words of the heart directly to him. Talk to him, and then listen with your whole being. Feel his energy whenever you're in need. Make a fire outdoors or simply speak to him through the flame of a candle and you will be able to spread his light and energy as you do the energy of Sun.

36. Source

*Even if I know no one, how can I feel alone in the city? The
wind is in my hair, my father Sun is shining on me, and my
feet are standing on my mother. And look around. Everywhere
in this city I am surrounded by my Grandfather Fire.*

Tayau (Alfredo Gonzales Ponciano)*

The large cities and metropolitan areas of the world are exciting
and alive with energy—each has a particular "feel" and quality, a
unique energy that is the result of the people who live in it, its
history, where it's located, and so forth. Every city is alive with its
own brand of movement, and life. Nevertheless, our lives in the
modern cities of this world most often leave little room for spending time in Nature. There are city dwellers who have never even
felt grass between their toes or soil in their hands. In addition, the
pace of city life can be frantic and the noise, congestion, buildings,
cars, and flashing lights can transform us into beings who live
completely disconnected from what is happening in the natural
world—even those of us who are able to access Nature.

Once on a trip to Mexico City I was very surprised to find one
of my Huichol Indian brothers from the mountains there as well,
visiting mutual friends. He was wearing his beautifully embroi-
dered traditional clothing, and although the weather was cold he
had made the five-day trip from his home with only one small
purselike bag and no jacket. He looked very out of place yet completely comfortable, and I remember asking him if he felt strange
and alone in such a huge, noisy, crowded place while his family,
community and the natural world he knew so well were so far
away. He simply laughed and said, "Everywhere in this city I am
surrounded by my Grandfather Fire. What do you think makes all

---

*Tayau (Alfredo Gonzales Ponciano), Huichol president of the Union of Jicareros
of Jalisco, personal conversation, Mexico City, 1998.

these lights work? What makes all these thousands of cars and trucks go? And Fire lives inside every one of these millions of people." I was astounded. I had been working in isolated areas of wilderness for years trying to develop my connection to the nierikas he was describing, and it had never occurred to me that they were here and alive in the city.

This is the discovery encouraged by the following practice, which should be performed in a metropolitan area in either daylight or at night.

Instructions for the Practice

1. Begin in the Fox Stance and state out loud your intention to be able to see the source of the power that animates all the beings and things of the city.

2. Start walking and look at everything and everyone you pass in a way that's similar to the perspective you use in Walk 5, Child's Eyes. See with new eyes all of the manifestations of power and energy around you.

3. At the same time, try to look deeper—into the source of what you see. Look at each thing or being in a way that penetrates to its very core. See the essence and energy that moves everything that crosses your path. Then move past the limits of sight and *feel* each manifestation of energy that you come upon. Spend some time exploring this state.

4. Next, as you walk, try to see the different manifestations of the five main nierikas in various forms around you. Maybe you can't see Sun because of the tall buildings, but you can probably see the shadows. You may not see Fire in his most literal form, but you may see him all around you in the form of thousands of car lights or traffic signals. You may not feel Wind but you may see many different beings breathing in the air. Water might not be visible in the form of a brook or pond, but each of the human

beings around you is made up of about 60 percent water. And while Earth cannot be seen or felt under your feet, she is present in the fruits, vegetables, and flowers for sale on the street and in the food served in restaurants. The nierikas are always with us, even in the biggest cities. They are the source of life in everything.

Comments on the Practice

Take the experience of this walk with you and use it again and again as you walk through life. If you can find the nierikas in the city, think how much more readily you will find them in the wilderness—you will never be alone. Once you have learned that the nierikas are always around you, they can provide an immeasurable source of strength to your life.

4

Walks of Connection to Animals, Trees, and Places of Power

ANIMALS

From elephants to whales, to big cats such as lions and tigers, to tiny finches and hummingbirds, animals are our companion beings on this planet and have an immense amount of knowledge that we can draw from. By connecting with animals we open up a huge book of wisdom as diverse in its teachings as the animal kingdom itself, a source of knowledge that is often forgotten but, with all its potential benefits, seems imperative to include in our modern lives.

Through the ages and within countless cultures, animals have been revered as gods and goddesses, mythical figures, and spirit beings. Ancient societies used animals and depictions of animals in all sorts of spiritual practices that are often misunderstood by modern society. But even today, though by and large we have lost our spiritual connection to animals, we can see clearly the beauty and majesty of the world's precious creatures.

One of the saddest results of modern culture, however, is our mistreatment of animals—every day we destroy their natural homes and take their lives to make room for new construction and the means to feed our never-ending material greed. Every day we raise and slaughter them on factory farms to feed our often unhealthy appetites. This is not to say that we should never build on the planet or eat meat, but there must be balance and thought in our actions and a consideration of the rights of those creatures who share this planet with us.

It is not too late, however, to regain balance in our relationships with our animal brothers and sisters, to restore our collective respect for all forms of creation. The Earthwalks in this section help toward this end, allowing you to open yourself to discovering and exploring our lost connection to the powerful animals that surround us, leading you to the wisdom and energy they can offer.

37. Breakthrough

*While you're outdoors, observe an animal closely. Follow it as
it moves. See how nature has expressed itself uniquely in this
animal. Become quiet within your mind, so that you can
become sensitively aware of the animal's essence. Mentally
offer your appreciative thoughts to the animal. Listen.*

JOSEPH CORNELL*

A simple way to discover the magic of animals is to allow yourself
to be available to their world and give yourself over to their lead.
This is how many ancient traditions initiated their shamans into
the knowledge of animal spirits.

Of primary importance to reestablishing our connection to our
animal brothers and sisters is our intentional desire to respect them.
Until we can truly see how magical and special they are, we won't
be able to relate to them at more than a superficial level. The kind
of appreciation required goes beyond simply being aware of their
beauty. Just as with humans, animals' appearances can provide only
clues as to what lies beneath—and often belie it. In the animal
kingdom many of the most important or resonant lessons can be
gleaned from "homely" or "ugly" creatures.

A perfect example of this is one of the birds I most respect, the
turkey vulture. Most would agree that this creature is not in the least
physically beautiful or appealing. But these birds serve an important
role in the balance of certain ecosystems, and upon connecting with
them you will discover much more about their world and ours. They
perceive in a way that is dramatically different from ours: They have
developed the ability to perceive energy currents as they move and
spiral in endless circles all around us and into the heavens. They are
also remarkable for their excellent and beautiful flying skills—they

---

*Joseph Cornell, *Listening to Nature* (Nevada City, Calif.: Dawn Publications,
1987).

soar with grace and fluidity that seem to run counter to their awkward appearance, but remain exceptionally connected to the energy of Earth as well as to the sky. In fact, they have such a solid connection to Earth that they nest, lay their eggs, and raise their young on the ground. In this way the energy of the soil, roots of trees, and rock becomes part of their being from their first moments of life and gives them a particular gift of vision as they navigate the sky.

Connecting with a vulture leads to a powerful experience of perception and awareness that, for some, belies the unassuming physical characteristics of this magical being. There are thousands of examples of similarly "unattractive" animals that have, like their more comely brother and sister creatures, the ability to reveal to us wondrous lessons.

Those people who lived in ancient societies regularly moved about in Nature, giving themselves the opportunities to connect with animals and their teachings and discovering how to retain their balance with other beings of the planet. What would our society be like if we were to allow ourselves to access this knowledge? With all the human-created wars, hate, destruction, brutality, hunger, and overpopulation throughout the world, what would the animals say if we gave them the chance to speak? This Earthwalk begins to answer these questions.

When you first begin learning how to listen to animals, it's important to start listening to those that naturally share our energy space. Approaching such unfamiliar and energetically powerful animals as jaguars and grizzly bears and rattlesnakes is both impractical and dangerous—not only would you have little chance of understanding what they are saying to you, but also this lack of understanding could cause you to approach them improperly, making such an encounter deadly for you and any people accompanying you.

Developing an ability to listen involves transforming and expanding both your energy and your perception to states closer to those of the animals around you. You can accomplish this by working on your connection to the animals' environment—learning through feelings and exploring the lessons of the habitat and what it means to be a part of it. Start by learning from the animals that don't feel compelled to run from you or predictably hide when you are around. These creatures are the companions of those you don't see, and by connecting with them you will be taking steps to connect with all the others. There is a reason that some don't run as far or hide as often.

Remember that the lessons you are supposed to receive will come to you through the proper animals in the proper place and at the proper time. Perhaps after you have broken through the barriers that separate you from other creatures of Earth and you become able to develop and nurture relationships with the ones appointed to teach you, you will be called to seek out others. At that point you may need to do some searching, but by then the search itself will have meaning and lessons and will be guided by forces that ensure the proper circumstances.

This walk involves merging your intention with the energy of the specific place where you are walking in order to call out the creatures that live there, and then asking these animals to share with you what you need to know.

Instructions for the Practice

1. Begin with Walk 1, Walk of Attention. After your thoughts are quiet, start recapitulating those moments in your life that have included animals, excluding pets. Simply let a memory come, feel it for a moment or two, and then move on. If you haven't had many experiences with animals, think of this day as a wonderful chance to fill this gap in your experience.

2. After you have recapitulated these events, stop walking, raise your arms, and state out loud to the animals of the world your desire to connect with them in a more meaningful way. This is your personal statement of intention—say all you wish, taking

all the time you need. Be sure to state what you will do to realize your connection, such as spending more time with animals or learning where the meat you eat comes from.

3. Next, be ready to receive whatever the creatures around you have to offer. Begin to walk very slowly until an animal first crosses your path, then observe this animal with all your being. Notice everything about it—the colors, patterns, and textures of its skin or fur, the size and shape of each of its body parts. Feel the magic that animates this creature and that is expressed through the form this animal takes.

4. Begin to breathe in the energy of this animal and try to perceive the world the way it does—see the surrounding environment through its eyes. As you do this, express to it through your feelings or soft words that you are trying to understand it and become a friend. Ask for help and then watch and learn from its actions, noticing how it moves and how it senses.

5. This next step depends upon what occurs between you and your new animal friend. If it has come and gone quickly, you might want to spend a few minutes reflecting on your encounter. It may be that you will have to wait for another occasion to continue your relationship. Or you may feel the call to keep walking with it or following behind it. If this is the case, then continue to observe every detail of its actions. When the moment comes to say good-bye, speak your farewell out loud and thank the creature and all its relations for giving you a chance to know them.

Comments on the Practice

If you are having trouble encountering animals in the wild, then you probably need to work more on your internal energy—go back and enjoy some of the previous walks in this book. More than likely the walks that you don't feel as attracted to are the ones that will be most beneficial to you. Remember to challenge yourself, especially with those practices that seem difficult or otherwise unattractive.

Step 1 of this practice is important for prompting the energy inside you to move in a specific way that relates to animals. By recapitulating your experiences pertaining to animals, you are opening an energetic door to them.

You should state in a very strong way your desire to connect with and learn from them. Remember to include in your statement the fact that you are offering your time and energy to learn. If you wish, you can even offer something concrete of your making that represents your desire to reconnect with your animal brothers, such as a drawing or handwork of some kind.

Remember that it is important to approach animals slowly and in a slightly roundabout way rather than walk directly to them. Some animals will be more approachable if you don't look at their eyes right away—it often helps to look down or away from them, which they perceive as a nonthreatening sign that you mean no harm.

Every time you walk after performing this particular practice, be open to the opportunity to continue a relationship with the animal you've encountered here—or find a new friend along your path. Use your feelings and not your rational mind to dictate how to proceed. You may not be able to understand the language of animals but at certain levels you can feel it—allow this to be your guide. It will take time to develop relationships with your animal friends. They may need to test your friendship before letting you into their world. Because each creature has a specific energy and unique lessons to give, as you develop and change, so will the animals that are part of your life. But whether you befriend a squirrel for some time or a fox or a deer, be sure you learn all you can.

38. Journey

Like the dream messages or the wind or whatever belongs to the
wild, the animal comes in its own time and place . . . The fantas-
tic, timeless, spaceless happening comes when it will: not because of
you. And that is what makes it so treasured. Curiosity in the
creature, quite as much as the human's wish to see the animal,
brings the two together. It is a convergence, in the same way that
the appearance of the dream is a convergence with the dreamer.
The observer, the dreamer, the creature, and the dream are all on
the same path. Without wilderness and without the great inner
psychic matrix, there are no such magical moments.

JANE HOLLISTER WHEELWRIGHT
AND LYNDA WHEELWRIGHT SCHMIDT*

Once you have begun to develop your relationships with specific
animals, you will find that there are unlimited ways to learn from
them. By reading their tracks, examining their scat, and watching
what they eat and where they sleep, you will grow familiar with
them and may even be able to predict their reaction to certain
situations. The journey of discovery has just begun. It is a challenging process, but ultimately they may become not just friends
but real companions as well.

To reach this pinnacle, you must learn to focus your energy in
a way that allows you to shift your perception to a place closer to
theirs, to join with their spirit on a number of levels so that, for
instance, each of you can glimpse the others' feelings or concerns.
At the highest levels of connection, a person and an animal become one.

This technique of connecting with the spirit of an animal is an

---

*Jane Hollister Wheelwright and Lynda Wheelwright Schmidt, *The Long Shore:
A Psychological Experience of the Wilderness* (San Francisco: Sierra Club Books,
1991).

ancient and extremely powerful one but is not readily accessible unless you have developed your energy and abilities to a level that enables you to enter into other worlds of perception. The descendants of those ancient people who practiced this technique still carry on this tradition today, spending whole lifetimes developing their energy toward reaching a state of oneness with members of the animal kingdom. In this effort, such men and women endure years of periodic fasting, vision questing, pilgrimages, abstinence from sexual relations, isolation from friends and family, and frequent ceremonies and prayer.

Most of us, of course, are not prepared to make the sacrifices necessary to connect at this level and do not feel the need to make such a life choice. But for whatever life choice you do make, your animal companions can help you enormously if they are called to do so.

It's helpful to know at the outset that attention plays an important role in any relationship with an animal companion—all of the walks you have performed up to this point have developed your attention. Likewise, learning to walk with the nierikas helps with this practice—the animals walk with the nierikas each day.

Instructions for the Practice

1. Be sure that you and your animal companion have developed a relationship characterized by a feeling of mutual trust and comfort when you are in each other's company. Some signs that your animal trusts you include its willingness to stay in your proximity rather than running away, and that it lies down, rests, or even sleeps while knowing you are close by.

2. You yourself can decide when and how to begin this practice. If you have been working with other Earthwalks in this book and have developed a relationship with your animal companion, you will know when to begin—circumstances and energy build in such a way that timing becomes clear. Perhaps you have discovered a new aspect of your companion that you never noticed

before, or you might find one of its brothers sick or dying, or perhaps you find a baby of your companion, lost and hungry. Whatever sign manifests itself, continue behaving with your companion as you have up to this point. To have developed your relationship thus far indicates that your actions are both appropriate and fruitful. Always remember, however, to be patient and safe.

3. Once you have decided it is time to begin, start walking with your animal companion as dictated by your feelings. Your companion will determine whether this walk will require you to travel—maybe even run—over great distances or to move merely in the realm of perception while covering very little physical ground. When the moment is right, ask your animal companion, with energetic intention that may or may not be voiced in words, to guide you and teach you.

4. Once the journey with your animal companion commences, you must give in wholly to the experience. For example, I have walked with companion deer for a mile or so and then stopped and stayed in the same small area for many hours as they slept and groomed, but have also shared an intense experience that lasted only a few seconds when my groundhog friend showed me how he runs as fast as he can from one hole to the next to avoid anyone catching him. Try not to think about what the experience should be—simply open yourself to it fully and let it happen.

5. Only after your experience ends will you be able to know what happened. Of course, you might not remember it at all except for a vague feeling that something special occurred. You may feel that you've just awakened from a dream, or you may find yourself in a physical location that is far from where you started your walk. All of these situations are typical when you are dealing with the world on an energetic or spiritual level.

Comments on the Practice

This Earthwalk can translate into an unlimited number of experiences. My most recent, for instance, occurred with a particular breed of large bird. One day, after years of spending time with these birds and, with their permission, visiting their young, I found one of their elders on the ground, unable to fly anymore. Though witnessing this made me quite sad, I knew this creature was simply finishing his part of the cycle that we are all connected to. I stayed with him all that day because I felt this creature had something to share with me—and as night approached, I took a magical journey with this new friend so near the end of his life. While sitting with him for many hours that day, my thoughts had silenced so much that the wings of my perception opened, and as he began to hop down the mountain—remember, he couldn't fly—I walked behind him.

As we traveled I perceived that we merged and he took me up into the sky with him, showing me how he used to view the world when he could fly and pointing out many remarkable things about the landscape. When our journey together had finished and we were back on the ground, he looked me in the eye and then hopped away down the mountain. I never saw him again and I never found his remains—but when I came back to that same spot the next day and began to follow the path he had taken as he hopped away from me the night before, I found instead a mother bird of the same breed and the two eggs she was caring for. I have never forgotten this experience and I still learn from it and apply it to my life today.

As you might guess, I kept an eye on the mother and the eggs, and although one of the chicks died at an early age, the other is my friend and I still see it from time to time and once in a while we fly together. Since the day of my journey with the old bird I have had a new level of connection with birds of this kind and especially the ones that live on that same mountain. Whenever I go there, I consider it a visit with my relatives, which gives me feelings of family, strength, and connection to the natural world. In these ways my experiences with the old bird and its friends and relations have added to and enriched my life. It is well worth the effort and time required to make these kinds of connections and I sincerely wish that everyone who reads these words will achieve something similar with an animal companion.

TREES

Trees have always played an important part in the lives of human beings, expressing through their actions the life-giving breath of Earth, and supplying beauty, majesty, and diversity to the landscape of the world while remaining rooted in eternal connection to the forces of Nature. We are intimately connected to trees through our sacred reciprocal relationship of breath—they supply us with the oxygen we need and we return the carbon dioxide they require. Trees generously give us the materials to make our furniture, houses, newspapers, and many other products. They provide shade, food, and shelter for countless creatures and hold a powerful and important place in the cycle of life and death. But their purposes are not only utilitarian—through help from Wind they make music and sing beautiful songs, and where they stand together in the deepest groves and forests, they hold the secrets and mysteries of the natural world with silent vigilance and nobility.

We might ask ourselves why we so recklessly sacrifice these beings to our wasteful habits and desires. It is through ignorance of the delicate balance in the cycle of life and of the necessity of replenishing Earth's energy. In the words of Richard St. Barbe Baker, "If a man loses one-third of his skin, he dies. If a tree loses one-third of its bark, it dies. Would it not be reasonable to suggest that if the Earth loses more than a third of its green mantle and tree cover, it will assuredly die?"* We all recognize that there is a complex web of people's economic dependencies that must be addressed as we form practical solutions for saving our brothers the trees. If each of us, as consumers of wood products, could develop

*Richard St. Barbe Baker, in William E. Marks, *The Holy Order of Water* (Great Barrington, Mass.: Bell Pond Books, 2001), 150.

and learn about our true feelings for these beloved beings as we engage in the process of sorting out priorities in this web, it would immeasurably help the trees and their needs.

In this Earthwalk you will reconnect to the power of the trees so that all of us can begin to alter our thoughtless selfishness with regard to these graceful citizens of the natural world and begin to value their many gifts. Our brothers the trees have much to share with those who take care that their place in the web of life is preserved.

39. Below and Above

The way we stand, you can see we have grown up this way together, out of the same soil, with the same rains, leaning in the same way towards the Sun. See how we lean together in the same direction. How the dead limbs of one of us rest in the branches of another. How those branches have grown around the limbs. How the two are insepa- rable. . . . And how we are each purpose, how each cell, how light and soil are in us, how we are in the soil, how we are in the air, how we are both infinitesimal and great and how we stand, each alone, yet none of us separable, none of us beautiful when separate but all exquisite as we stand, each moment heeded in this cycle, no detail unlovely.

SUSAN GRIFFIN*

For this walk it is best to be in a wooded area where you can ex- plore the energy of trees of different types and ages.

Instructions for the Practice

1. Begin with Walk 1, Walk of Attention, and continue it for sev- eral minutes.

---

*Susan Griffin, *Women and Nature: The Roaring Inside Her* (San Francisco: Sierra Club Books, 1978).

As you move, sense the overall collective energy of the trees that surround you. Feel the forest: its age and level of well-being, the season of its life and the mood it is in. Feel the level of motion the current season of the year brings and manifests through the energy of the plants and trees—is the forest busy blossoming into spring or slowing down for winter? Is Wind joining with the woods in a raging chorus of sound or silently whispering? Feel all that is happening and allow your energy to match your surroundings.

2. Gradually as you walk, become aware of the feeling of community in the forest. Note how the different kinds of trees live together in harmony. Notice the birds as they come and go, the insects on the ground, in the air, and living in the trees. See the fungi and molds, the fallen leaves and branches, and the carcasses of trees, once alive, that have fallen back to Earth to be recycled. Be aware that the community around you represents an integral part of the cycle of Nature and the balance and harmony within the natural world.

3. Walk until you encounter a tree for which you feel a special affinity. Stand beside it and without touching it ask permission to feel its energy and nierika. Listen for the answer, and if the tree approves, wrap your arms around its trunk. If this tree is not receptive to your request, then simply ask another. As you embrace the tree, feel its energy and try to meld yours with it. The energy of trees moves in a way that's quite different from human energy—its speed is much slower. Sense the roots of the tree running deep into Mother Earth and try to extend your energy to the roots as well—even into the tiniest and deepest root hairs. Feel the profound energy and love that Earth provides the tree and how the tree responds by growing and blossoming.

4. Now move your energy up the trunk and feel the strength and power of the body of the tree. The wood is a live manifestation of the power and love of Earth, a treasure of Nature holding the force of slow and thoughtful knowledge. Keep moving your energy and awareness up to the top of the tree and out through all the branches, as you feel yourself extending up and out, reaching for the life-giving light of the sun. Take in Wind and Sun as you take in the view from the top of the tree. The sea of life swells around the tree though it never moves from this spot—it is rooted to Earth, weathering every storm. Sense fully how the tree is part of the great cycle of life and how it will return to and replenish Earth when its job here is done.

5. When you have thoroughly explored, let go of the tree and thank it for all the gifts that it and its relations provide us. Reassure it that you will not forget your responsibility to protect all trees and use their gifts with respect and reverence.

6. Begin to walk again, stopping to explore other types of trees in different areas so that you can receive their diverse messages. An old, large tree standing in a quiet valley next to a stream will have something different to say than a scrubby, lithe tree living at the top of a high windy ridge or one that lives next to a new housing development.

Comments on the Practice

Try connecting to trees when you visit different areas and listen to what they have to say. There is no better way to feel the pulse of a place than through connection with its trees and other growing things. Although they are, unfortunately, quite rare, visiting an old-growth forest can be a profound experience, a way of connecting with some of the oldest beings on the planet. Living within Great Basin National Park in Nevada is a bristlecone pine that is five thousand years old! And it is young compared to a shrub in

Australia that has been living since the Stone Age. It is relatively easy to find out if there are old-growth forests in your state or in an area you'll be visiting: Contact the state's Park Service, or visit www.old-growth.org. Remember, no matter what type of tree you are visiting, always ask its permission before touching it, climbing it, or removing its fruit.

Whenever you plan to build a fire, always use wood that has fallen from a tree rather than cutting live branches. Remember that you are a visitor in the forest—walk gently and considerately and the trees will embrace you and welcome you to their home.

PLACES OF POWER

There exist many wondrous places on the planet where high concentrations of energy are gathered in specific forms, affording us the opportunity to discover and access the potent knowledge carried in such remarkable energetic configurations. Some of these places correspond to geological locations of physically measurable magnetic energy resulting from Mother Earth's relationship to other heavenly bodies, some have been created by humans as an expression of energetic intention, and some are areas whose reason for existing remains completely mysterious. Along with these sites there are places where humans have harnessed existing energetic power and channeled it by erecting on-site places of worship, monuments, and even entire cities so that both the natural power of place and the power of intention exist simultaneously.

In the following Earthwalks, you will explore both natural and man-made places of power in order to learn what they may have to teach us and how we may begin to use the nierika they possess.

40. Encounter

We may discover that altered states at sites with special properties allow entry to highly specialized orders of consciousness which give direct access to the energy body of the Earth.

Paul Devereaux*

This practice should be performed only in a natural place where there is no evidence of the powerful intention created by humans in the form of places of worship or archaeological ruins.

Paul Devereaux, *Earthmind: A Modern Adventure in Ancient Wisdom* (Rochester, Vt.: Destiny Books, 1992).

The natural world is filled with mysteries that lie hidden within its very fabric. Streams, rivers, canyons, deserts, mountains, and forests each contain a unique power that is a cumulative product of its individual component parts. In connecting to a single tree, you can sense the energy nurtured by the tree's component roots connecting it to the soil and limbs that receive energy directly from the sun. Now if this tree, with its individual energy, is part of a forest of thousands of trees, each with its own energy, the result is a formidable amount of power. Adding in the energy of all the other beings that inhabit this forest—animals, plants, insects— means the end product is even more total energy. Finally, figure in the power of the nierikas—Sun, Water, Wind, Earth, and Fire— that contribute the energy necessary for the growth and survival of the forest and it's easy to see that this forest has a unique energetic quality and awesome power, which can easily be felt if you are available to it.

There are many places on the planet that hold even more energy than a forest like the one described above—power that astounds and defies explanation, that produces an "aliveness," a nierika that seems like a living being, as real as you and I. How such places originated, no one knows—but their power most certainly can be felt.

Developing a relationship with these places of power is the goal of this Earthwalk. You will learn to open yourself to the unique energy and lessons of such a place and, in turn, give your personal energy to it.

Because the power of Nature can sometimes be overwhelming, if your intention is to connect with this power, you must do so in an appropriate way and with the proper attitude: Remain focused on what you are doing and keep your mood light. Be attentive to what is happening and what you are feeling at all times. And remember that just as do the nierikas, the powers in these places will communicate in unusual ways—be ready to seize the experience. What a shame it is that so many people pass through powerful places like the Grand Canyon and the Smoky Mountains (to name just two) only seeing the beauty around them but never attending to and absorbing the energy and mysteries that live there!

Instructions for the Practice

1. By now you have developed to some extent your ability to feel the energy from your natural surroundings, which means you may well know when you are entering a special place of power. When this happens, the first thing to do is relax and breathe. Next, create the proper atmosphere for your encounter with this power by removing all nonessential distractions: If there are other people around who don't share your mission, try to move from them physically or at least block their energy from affecting you by treating their sounds with respect but not allowing them dominating importance.

2. Once you are ready, begin by calling to the power of the place: With arms outstretched and in a strong voice, tell the power that you are visiting, that you can feel its presence, and that you wish to learn. In order to enter into a healthy exchange with this energy, you must offer to use any knowledge or gifts you receive in a way that will spread the light of Father Sun and the love of Mother Earth. Along with this you may offer whatever else you feel is appropriate. (See part 5, Offering and Vision, for some suggestions.)

3. Begin walking with the feeling that you have nothing covering you. You can perform this practice without clothing, but with or without, the most important thing is the *feeling* that there is nothing between you and the great power and mystery around you. This sense is helped by imagining that you are bare to the world—even to the point that you have no skin. All your thoughts of self have fallen away, all your physical feelings have been shed, even the very skin from your body has been sloughed

off to reveal the flesh of your soul. This feeling of complete nakedness will produce in you a shiver of power in the depths of
your being, which comes not from being cold but from opening
yourself fully. When this occurs, you are ready to receive. Adjust
your breathing so that the inhalation is the beginning and strongest part of your breath while the exhalation remains normal—
this places emphasis on drawing in energy with each breath.

4. Walk slowly as your flesh absorbs every nuance of energy and
power sent to you by your surroundings. Openly receive the
messages of the place and merge with them. Feel the quality of
the energy—is it soft or harsh, friendly or frightening, fresh or
old? Listen for the silent meaning of what you receive.

5. When you have finished receiving, you must cover yourself in
order to face the world again—the world of people is much too
harsh to walk around in this state of "nakedness." Leave the
area where you have been working and slowly return to your
usual awareness. If you remember specifics about your walk or
the lessons you received, write them down right away. In these
notes you should not attempt to explain what you experienced;
their purpose is to help you remember the moments and realize
the offering you made at the beginning of your walk.

Comments on the Practice

It often happens that once you have experienced the profound
effects of connecting with the nierika of a natural place of power,
whether deeply or superficially, you will sense, either instantly or
some time afterward, a sort of magnetic pull to other places of
power. I am convinced that this is one way Earth can connect with
us. The large numbers of people who flock to national parks, the
resurgence of Nature-based spirituality, and the growth of eco-
tourism and other Nature-oriented activities are all evidence of
this. Earth is surely calling us—the more deeply we are able to
listen, the more we will be able to understand.

41. Sphere

Power spots tend to amplify the frequency of your own energy field and energize your existing thoughts and emotions. Spiritually oriented people have built temples and churches over large power spots, wishing to amplify inspired thoughts and emotions of a spiritual nature. The people who flock to these spots contribute to the collective feeling that is already there, making the spot more and more powerful and oriented with a particular flavor. . . . You need to be careful what state you are in before entering into the sphere of influence of such a spot . . . it is a good idea to prepare yourself by centering and calming yourself before knowingly going to a power spot.

José Stevens and Lena Stevens*

Use this Earthwalk in places of power that are known to be sites of enormous energy by the presence of human-built monuments or other construction, either physical or energetic, as a result of the intention of humans who have lived, worked, or worshiped there. It's important to note that there are untold numbers of places where humans have forged their intention but where the physical remains of their presence is not readily visible. Sometimes we encounter the power of such a place in Nature but are not aware of where it came from or why it is present. Places where ancient ceremonies were held, hidden burial sites, known sites that have not yet been excavated by archaeologists, and so forth are places where a strong power cultivated by people from the past may still linger. In most cases these places should be avoided: You could suffer energetic damage as a result of powerful foreign energy penetrating yours. Unless you have a specific reason for exploring such places, it is probably best to steer clear of them.

Known places of power such as pyramids and temples and other

---

*José Stevens and Lena Stevens, *Secrets of Shamanism: Tapping the Spirit Within You* (New York: Avon Books, 1988).

places of worship or ceremony should also be approached with caution once you have opened yourself to relating to the world at an energetic level. These places pose little threat to those who have not opened themselves to their deeper energetic capacity, but remember that through all of the various Earthwalks you have experienced up to this point, you have been removing the layers of ego-driven self-importance that block the perception of the movement of energy and nierika. Now that you are more open, you are also more sensitive. This doesn't mean that you shouldn't explore man-made places of power—just make sure that you remain particularly focused on what it is you're doing there. And proceed appropriately, following the steps of this Earthwalk.

These types of powerful places can be sources of wonder and mystery. The forces of energy that were needed to construct buildings or ceremonial sites or monuments such as pyramids and the reasons behind their construction offer you opportunities for a variety of experiences. While they can be very positive sources of power, their energy can also be volatile and terrifying depending upon the mood and rationale of those who built them and the activities for which they were used—and, most important, how you take in the energy you receive. You can explore these places in such a way that you are able to learn and protect your energy at the same time.

Instructions for the Practice

1. When walking into a location that is a known place of power— or if you ever become aware that you are encountering one unknown to you—you should first take a step backward, close your eyes, and breathe in a way that isolates your energy and power from the rest of the world (exhaling becomes the more forceful part of your breath and inhaling becomes relatively shallow).

2. Before opening your eyes, envelop yourself with your energy: Feel and envision your energy as a definite spherical body that surrounds you. This energy field has a definite boundary that is

approximately an arm's length away from your body, creating for you a feeling that is quite opposite that of Walk 40, Encounter, in which you opened yourself unconditionally to the energy and power around you. In this practice, the boundary determines where your energy goes, which protects you from being caught in the intentions of outside forces.

3. Open your eyes and begin walking, making sure your energy remains within your sphere. This involves allowing outside energy, feelings, and sensations to contact your sphere so that you may experience them, but not entering into an actual exchange with them. Note that it is entirely possible to receive the feelings, energy, and mood of a place of power without exchanging energy with it.

4. If, however, at some moment during your walk you feel confident enough about a certain place to make yourself available for an energy exchange, then use a technique similar to that used in Walk 40—but be aware, before making such a decision, that the intention cultivated by humans is rarely as pure as the love felt from Nature.

5. If you feel threatened by a place of power at any time during your visit, you must keep your composure and immediately block any exchange of energy. This could be accomplished by simply exhaling deeply, but it may be that you have to physically leave the site. If this is necessary, don't dwell on it, allowing your thoughts to run in a million directions as to how or why things occurred as they did. Instead, immediately involve yourself in an energetic activity and feel glad that you were able to pass safely through a difficult energetic situation.

Comments on the Practice

It can take some time to cultivate the sense that your energy forms a sphere around your body, and even when you've accomplished this there is no guarantee of what will happen when you enter a place of powerful energy. A great deal of the sphere's success has to do with your internal feelings, your mood, and your energy level. I have performed this Earthwalk countless times but each time my experience has been different.

The first time I went to the ancient Toltec city of Tula in central Mexico, I walked into the archaeological zone after having performed months of exercises in the wilderness to clear myself of the negative events in my past. You could say that I was wide open to receiving the fresh, new world. I didn't know the sphere technique—and even if I did, I wouldn't have been aware of any reason to use it. After quickly walking around the archaeological site and up and down the pyramids with no real goal other than to "site see," I began to feel lightheaded. I kept walking, however, and gradually felt sick to my stomach. Finally, I experienced a pressure so strong that it seemed to be pushing on my entire body from the outside—and I had to leave. I was practically running away from the site at that point. The whole intense visit to that place lasted only about a half hour.

The next time I visited I was familiar with protecting my energy within the sphere around my body. I was able to explore the whole site inside and out for a whole day. During that visit I was very strong about my intention not to be affected by the place, so even though I explored it, I didn't discover very much.

The third time I visited Tula I walked with my sphere the whole time but was more relaxed and confident. The result was that I was able to begin to feel the energy and secrets of the place while remaining apart and safe from its energetic intention.

An interesting point is that power places influenced or constructed by man usually reveal more Nature-based energy if they were created prior to the seventeenth century, or the beginning of the Age of Reason. Sites that contain stone circles or petroglyphs or mounds can connect us in a very real way to cultures that lived close to Earth. When visiting these sites, remember that the use of space reveals a great deal about the worldview of its creators. Kivas, for example, which are circular ceremonial chambers built into the ground, indicate a reverence for Earth and the connection to her.

42. Split

We live in the place of duality called Omeyocan by the ancient Toltecs. Although we are surrounded by it at every moment, modern people require special training to learn to perceive both sides of the duality that reside in this world.

VICTOR SANCHEZ*

This Earthwalk is designed for places of power familiar to you that you know do not affect you adversely and that you wish to explore in a deep way. It can be used in man-made or natural places of power and employs a technique that focuses your attention on two specific aspects of your perception and on the physical body.

Because places of power contain high quantities of energy and intention that together make them strongly magical places, and at the same time feature impressive or even spectacular scenery that makes them places that are much appreciated by those who are energetically attuned on only the most superficial level, they are perfectly suited for this walk. This practice can, however, be performed anywhere and at any time to discover the intricacies of a specific place or area.

Instructions for the Practice

1. Begin in the Fox Stance, blocking your vision from your left eye by covering it with your left hand. As you start walking, examine your physical surroundings with your right eye and the whole right side of your body, noticing only the physical,

---

*Victor Sanchez, personal conversation, Teotihuacán, Mexico, 1997.

tangible features of the area. Examine colors, shapes, scents, noises, textures, patterns, light, and shadow, but don't engage the feelings the place produces. Use only simple and direct observation relating to the exploration of your senses. Continue in this way for ten minutes.

2. Next, remove your left hand from your left eye and place your right hand over your right eye, obscuring that side of your vision. Continue walking and with your left eye and the whole left side of your body "feel" your surroundings, moving beneath the surface of the physical and tangible and using soft glances and your energy to uncover what lies beneath. What emotions and sensations does this particular place invoke? How do the individual physical characteristics of this place come together to form its unique energy and feeling? This is its magic, its nierika. Continue in this way until you have fully explored the area.

3. Remove your right hand so that you can once again see with both eyes and begin walking slowly. As you move, focus on using your right eye and right side as you did in step 1, to explore this place with your physical senses, and at the same time use your left eye and left side as you did in step 2, to explore the mystery and magic around you. Continue walking in this way, employing both awarenesses at the same time. Eventually you will feel as though you are split in two—but this is quite normal. The ancient people who created this technique in Teotihuacán, Mexico, were very practiced at splitting themselves in two to foster clearer focus within each awareness. After a time it will become apparent that you can discover much more than you would through usual sight and awareness.

Comments on the Practice

Continue walking with this dual vision for as long as is necessary to fully explore a place of power. If you should lose focus at any time, especially when learning this technique, simply return to walking with first the left eye covered and then the right eye covered to refocus your attention.

While, for ease of explanation, I have referred to the right eye and left eye corresponding to tangible and magical perception, respectively, it is actually more accurate to view the tangible world of the senses with your dominant eye and the magical world with the other eye. Usually the dominant eye is the one on the same side of the body as the hand you use for writing, but to be certain, you can take this simple test:

Stretch your arms out in front of you at eye level and with your index fingers and thumbs make a triangle that you can look through. Center this triangle on an identifiable object, making sure your arms remain outstretched. Now close one eye and look at the object through the triangle. Is it still in the center of the triangle? Open that eye, close the other, and look again. Is the object in the center of the triangle? The eye that sees the object in the center is your dominant eye and the one you should use to view the tangible; the other eye should be used to view the magical world.

5

Walks of Offering
and Vision

OFFERING AND VISION

An offering is a potent form of communication and gift of energy that can give power and meaning to our actions. It can make our intention clear, add force and direction to guide us down the path we have chosen, and communicate our desires and dreams to the nierikas and other forms of energy.

The Earthwalks that you have performed up to now have directly or indirectly placed you in a position of offering. By simply walking with the intention of reuniting with the world of Nature you have offered a part of yourself to the Great Mystery. Opening yourself in this way is powerful medicine for the soul but is only one of many forms of offering that exist to be used as you continue down the path of self-improvement and Earth healing.

The range of possibilities for offerings is as wide as you can imagine. They can include any part of yourself or anything that your creativity decides to release to the universe. They run the gamut from fasting for a period of time to giving a simple embrace, and only circumstances can dictate the proper offering for a given situation. Open your heart and you will know what to offer.

The following offerings are meant to complement the Earthwalks included in this book and your journey to reunite with Earth. These practices don't need to be performed exactly as they are written, but instead can serve as guides to lead you to your own most meaningful offerings. One of the most meaningful offerings we can make is to place ourselves directly into the arms of Nature for periods of time in order to receive a vision from the nierikas that pertains to our current life. In doing this we allow Earth to help direct our daily actions and life path.

43. Seasons of Change

*Live in each season as it passes; breathe the air, drink the drink,
taste the fruit, and resign yourself to the influence of each. Let
them be your only diet, drink and botanical medicines. Be
blown on by all the winds. Open your pores and bathe in all the
tides of nature, in all her streams and oceans, at all seasons.*

HENRY DAVID THOREAU*

Spring, summer, fall, and winter, which mark the passing of our year and the passage of time in the world of Nature, provide four perfect occasions for you to reflect on your life and make offerings to connect yourself with the cycles of Earth.

As members of modern society, most of us are not connected to our food sources in a way that allows us to associate them with the changing of the seasons and planting, growing, and harvesting. With air-conditioning, heat, and other forms of climate control in our living spaces, neither are we fully connected to the strong forces of weather brought about by the changing seasons. For these reasons, many of us don't celebrate the changes in the cycle of the seasons as fully as our ancestors did.

But even today there exist people who live close to Earth and celebrate the changing seasons with ceremonies and rituals that include offerings of intention for the following months and year. This Earthwalk accomplishes something similar: Your intention will be to carry out a walk in Nature once each season for the specific purpose of making an offering. Doing this will allow you to review your actions, make your commitments, and send your offerings to the nierikas while realizing the cycles of life to which we are intimately tied. You can perform this walk at any time during each of the four seasons, but doing so at the time of the solstice or

---

*Henry David Thoreau, *Wild Fruits* (New York: W. W. Norton, 2000).

equinox will add potency to your practice because of the proximity of these times to the moment that marks the specific change from one season to another. It can also strengthen your practice by allowing your offering to join the energy of the many people throughout the world who celebrate each solstice and equinox.

Instructions for the Practice

1. You must first shape and make an offering, through your own hands and heart, that relates to your current life. It may be a drawing, sculpture, or any type of handcraft, preferably made from materials that are nonpolluting and biodegradable, and should illustrate in some way the most important aspects of your current life such as concerns, dreams, successes and failures. Don't worry if you are not an artist—the only thing that matters is the level of feeling and energy you invest in your offering. Do your best, be creative, and allow your silent knowledge to express itself.

2. Transport your offering to the place where you will walk, but do not carry it in your hands—using a backpack is best because it allows your hands to be free. As you begin your walk, notice all the characteristics that the specific season brings. Nature shows her many faces throughout the year—observe the expression she wears in this particular season: What is the condition and color of the ground, trees, and plants? What is the temperature and what does the sky look like? Is it raining? Snowing? Is it windy or calm? How do the animals around you react to the seasonal atmosphere surrounding them? What new or different animals can you see? Do you seem to be missing some that are usually present? What is the quality of the sun's light? When does the sun arrive and when does it leave? What has Water been doing lately—is the ground damp or dry? Are the rivers high or low? Take your time—study the physical condition of the area around you and feel the energy that this season possesses.

3. Now remove your offering from your backpack and hold it in both hands in front of you. As you continue walking, review what it means to you, where you are in your life right now, and where you are going. Notice that this moment in your life is just like a season in Nature and that you are in a constant state of change and motion just as each season is.

4. At this moment, speak out loud and from the heart to Earth and the other nierikas your intentions for the season ahead. Share your hopes and dreams and what you plan to do to realize them. Speak so that the trees and other living beings around you can hear and witness your intentions.

5. At the proper moment, present your offering and leave it on the ground in a place that calls to you. As you walk away from it, review its meaning in your life.

Comments on the Practice

A wonderful place in which to leave your offering is your power place from Walk 33, Developing Reciprocity. Handmade offerings should be very specifically related to your life, future intentions, and dreams. My Huichol companions depict these through elaborate yarn paintings made by affixing various colors of yarn to a small wooden board covered with a thin layer of wax. Drawings like this are powerful ways to call the nierika of your offering and give to Earth in a way that transcends the verbal.

Use this walk to mark not only the changing of the seasons of Nature, but the changes in the seasons of your life as well. While this kind of ritual is absent from the lives of most people today, it is a simple and concrete way to connect with the natural world around you and the world inside yourself. As you perform this walk throughout many seasons, it will become a quiet celebration that you look forward to.

44. Giving Back

*Tree planting is a living, growing gift to the future unfolding in
the present. . . . Planting a tree, with a simple, family-created
ceremony, can be a wonderful family ritual for children and
parents . . . I was touched when I learned about [a] woman who
planted a tree in each place she had lived . . . I wistfully wished
that I had planted trees in the many places where our family has
lived through the years. If you are considering planting a tree, this
sign . . . [from] a nursery may be relevant to your decision:
The Best Time To Plant A Tree Is 15 Years Ago.
The Next Best Time Is Today!*

HOWARD CLINEBELL*

This walk, a practice of gift-giving to honor Mother Earth, is performed in a way that intentionally acknowledges humanity's loss of
direction with regard to living harmoniously with the natural world
and the beings that share it with us. Whether or not you feel you have
been a party to this imbalance, because you are a living, breathing
being on this planet it is important to look at what you may be
doing to hurt it and what you are doing to help it. Although decades
or maybe even lifetimes are needed to fully repair our relationship to
Nature, while we are working on ways to sustain our species without
destroying the environment there are many things you can do to help
counteract the effects of many years of waste.

This Earthwalk suggests making one intentional gift to Earth
as a symbolic gesture of your awareness and efforts to live in balance with her. Even if you have already done something like this,
do it again—we have a great deal of giving to do before we balance
our score with Nature.

---

*Howard Clinebell, *Ecotherapy: Healing Ourselves, Healing the Earth* (Minneapo-
lis: Fortress Press, 1996).

Instructions for the Practice

1. Begin by making a list of the things you can do to help Earth, including aspects of your life that you can change to live more in harmony with her. The list is endless, from the familiar and easily accomplished efforts such as increasing your recycling and walking rather than driving, to greater commitments such as organizing local wildlife surveys and volunteering for the board of an environmental group—but right now, the important thing is to choose a couple of commitments that you can honestly fulfill.

2. Now go to a nursery and purchase a small tree, making sure to select a variety that will have the best chance of surviving in the area where you will plant it.

3. Gather together your tree, any tools you will need to plant it, and your list and bring them with you to the place where you will begin your walk. This area might be your power place from Walk 33, Developing Reciprocity, or any other place to which you feel some connection and that is convenient. Because you will be carrying these things as you walk, it might be best to pack the smaller items in a backpack or canvas bag.

4. State out loud your intention for this Earthwalk and begin moving. As you walk, carry with you the feeling of love and the awareness of doing something positive for all the beings around you. Spread your good intentions and explore how it feels to be proactively helping Mother Nature with this good deed—in this moment, you are part of the solution.

5. Once you have reached the spot where you will plant the tree, first say some words of thanks to Mother Earth and the other nierikas and beings that surround you. Next, offer out loud the actions you have listed, making sure to tell Earth that this tree will be the symbol of your offering and that as it grows, so too will your heart and your efforts to protect her.

6. Plant your tree in the most responsible way you can, taking extra care with every detail in the process. When you are finished, be sure the area has been restored to its condition prior to your planting so that it appears as though the little tree was born there. After telling the tree that you are now its guardian and that you will love and care for it, say good-bye and plan when you will come back to check on it.

7. In the days, months, and years to come, spend time with your tree, nurture it, and notice its growth and changes. See it not merely as a symbol, but as your friend. Offerings of this nature are powerful; make sure that you fulfill your commitments and offerings.

Comments on the Practice

I recently returned to a place where my father and I had planted some trees over twenty-five years ago. In finding all the trees healthy and strong—and very tall—I was overwhelmed with tears of joy and thanks. I highly recommend that you share this Earthwalk with a child or other loved one. It can provide both of you with a moving and rich experience to share for many years to come.

If you are unsure of what you can do on a practical level to help Earth, there are many available resources to guide you, including environmental organizations, Web sites, and books. One of my favorite resources (although sometimes difficult to find) is *The Green Lifestyle Handbook: 1001 Ways You Can Heal the Earth*, edited by Jeremy Rifkin.

45. Walk for Vision

Ulu Temay, to find the answers you are searching for, to help
your people, you need to take your offerings and make your
sacrifices, to the ocean and the other sacred places. You have to
go to the sacred mountain five times in five years and seek the
visions waiting for you. You must start right now.

MARAKAME DIONICIO*

This, the last walking practice in this book, requires you to use the energy and lessons you have gained from all previous walks to help you as you seek and ultimately find a vision for your current life. You have been preparing for this practice since your very first Earthwalk. The walks of attention have taught you how to focus your attention on the elements of Nature in ways that, while they may have been alien to you, have assisted you in honing this discipline. You have walked together with other human beings to help forge for yourself a new and improved connection to groups of people. Through walks with the nierikas you have begun to develop a reciprocal relationship with the most powerful forms of energy in our world, which will be a continuing source of knowledge to you as you walk your life path. You have taken the trail back to the home of your animal brothers and sisters and now have new friends and companions to visit wherever you go in Nature. You have visited places of power and felt the workings of their magic and mystery, which have been, in many cases, affecting humans and Nature for centuries and even millennia. And finally, through sharing your heart in walks of offering, you have

---

*Marakame Dionicio (Huichol healer and shaman who sings the voice of the Fire), personal conversation while replacing the straw and wood roof of the community's *rirriki* (sacred house that holds their offerings), which is done after every five-year cycle, Cuexcomatitlán, Mexico, 2000. (Ulu Temay is the Huichol name given me by Dionicio; it means "ray of the Sun.")

entered the energy exchange of the universe and have helped to illuminate the world.

Now it is time to walk for vision from that space between worlds where power lives and dreaming and consciousness are one. Your offering in this walk will be your very self as you carry out this practice with impeccable preparation, attention, and awareness, and a great deal of heart. When the moment is right you will call to the nierikas for your vision and be ready to receive what they offer.

The structure of this practice is much looser and less directive than that of the other walks in this book—it is up to you to fill in its important logistical aspects. If you are a person accustomed to being outdoors, camping, and hiking for long periods, you may wish to extend this walk to two or three days. In the interest of safety for those not ready for an extensive trip alone in the wilderness, the walk is presented in its minimal but still very effective form.

In this walk you will use all the practices you have performed up to now in one full day of walking, from sunrise to sunset. Fasting and solitude can add to the power of your experience; however, please note that fasting is not a requirement for this practice and should not be observed by anyone whose physical health could be jeopardized by eliminating food intake for any period of time. Accessing all that you have learned in previous walks will serve to place you in a state of being that is quite separate from your everyday state and in this way will ready your perception to receive your vision.

The location of your walk is extremely important. Before planning your walking route, please assess honestly these skills and your fitness level. Be aware that because you will begin your walk at sunrise and end at sunset, you will be spending some time in the dark or near-dark. You can walk with or without a path to follow depending upon your outdoor skills. The ideal course for your walk is a large loop so that you can arrive at sunset where you began early in the day. You may also estimate approximately how far you can walk in one day, plan your route, and have someone pick you up at the end. Whichever course plan works best for you, please make sure that someone knows where you will be walking in case of difficulties or an emergency.

You will need some very basic equipment and supplies: A comfortable pair of shoes or boots is a must, as are clothes that are appropriate for the season and climate (remember that weather conditions may change as you travel—especially if your route involves an increase in altitude from your starting point to your end point). You will need to bring enough water—be sure to overestimate rather than underestimate the quantity—and a flashlight, and carry your items in a backpack. You may also take along any offerings you wish to give during the day, this book to use as a reference, and a pad and pencil to write any notes on insights you receive.

If fasting is an option for you, consider doing so the entire length of your walk until your return, after which you can eat a light meal. Fasting places you even further from your usual state of being and routine and, through creating a state of emptiness, allows your energy to be even more receptive. If fasting is not advisable for you or is not something you choose to make part of your experience, then by all means bring along some rations such as fruit or nuts.

Instructions for the Practice

1. Once you've made all your preparations, arrive at the starting place of your walk just before sunrise. Greet Father Sun with Walk 25, Sunrise, or something similar, and ask him to guide and protect you.

2. Begin walking along your preplanned route. As you travel, explore all the practices you have experienced up to now and try the ones you haven't yet performed. Use the walks of attention, transform yourself, walk barefoot, walk silently, peer into the shadows, and communicate with the beings around you and

with the nierikas. Make offerings and rejoice at being alive on this marvelous planet in this unique time and place. Stop and rest, if you need to, and if you experience any emotional difficulties as you walk, place your hands on Earth, draw in her energy, and talk to her.

3. Throughout your day, pay close attention to all that happens to you and the way you interact with your environment and yourself. Watch for any messages from the natural world and for your own internal signals. It is very common during an experience like this to receive songs or poems—if such things present themselves to you, stop and write them down so that you will be able to keep them in your memory. And be aware that though you will be calling for a vision during your walk, you may well receive one before your call or several throughout the day. Keep in mind that in the time of your first Earthwalk to this moment, you have succeeded in opening an energetic door. Stating your intention for this practice and proceeding to carry it out can be likened to walking through that door into the Great Mystery. Everything that happens to you during this day comes from that world. Anything is possible—embrace it! This is your chance!

4. When the day begins to wane and the shadows become long, it is time for you to call for your vision. As you walk, begin to recapitulate the important moments of all the walks you have performed: Recall what you have learned and what you have achieved. Call upon the energy and strength that these moments have given you. Envision yourself as you are—you are a magical being, alive and filled with the energy of Sun and Earth, a sphere of luminosity.

5. As sunset approaches, call for your vision (you will discover the exact place and time): Raise your arms and your voice to the heavens and speak to the nierikas, asking them for a vision to guide your current life. Speak words that come from your open

heart and not from your rational mind—and remember that your words are used only to move energy.

6. The moment to receive arrives when you have finished calling. Do whatever it is that feels right to do. If you are not sure, then simply drop to your knees and listen and watch. Remember that this vision will probably come in an unexpected form—it likely will have nothing at all to do with seeing, despite its name, and will have more to do with feelings and energy.

7. After you have received (again, you will know the exact time), thank the nierikas for keeping you safe and sharing their gifts. Be especially attentive to what is happening inside of you and around you as you complete your journey and prepare to return to your daily life—often visions reveal themselves after you've left the place of your call.

Comments on the Practice

This Earthwalk, which is similar to what some American Indian tribes would call a medicine walk, is just one of many ways for acquiring a vision while traveling alone in the wilderness. Once you have completed this walk for the first time, you will have available to you a powerful tool of vision seeking, one that you can use periodically as you travel through life. As you become more and more familiar with the process of learning and receiving from the natural world, you will develop your own approach to receiving the visions that Earth holds for you. We humans seem destined to veer at times from the path of right living. When we have strayed, a walk for vision is one of the best ways to help us return to the proper path.

Final Comments

I simply cannot stress enough the value of experiencing and not merely reading about the Earthwalks outlined here. The insights gleaned through physically and psychically interacting with the spirit of Nature are richer and deeper than anything we could read about, talk about, or even imagine. These insights are needed now more than ever as we embark on the task of transforming our acquisitive civilization into one that lives in harmony with Earth.

The impetus needed to perform this great task must be found in the hearts and minds of modern people, whose greatest pathology is the rejection of their place within the balanced life systems of the planet. But we cannot rely solely on our contemporary culture for the answers to this illness. Our great technological advances have failed us by creating a society dependent on the exploitation of natural resources, and our contemporary mainstream religions have failed to adequately promote the sacredness of Earth. In short, most of our modern institutions can't be trusted to deliver us from our current situation because they are precisely what have brought us here.

For humanity to live harmoniously with Earth we must find our niche within her living systems and exist within her boundaries just as all other living things do—and just as ancient and surviving Nature-based cultures do.

The ancient human cultures that still live separate from the modern world must not be overlooked as we search for ways to make our society more viable. People who don't depend on trucks and planes to bring them food, don't drive cars to and from work, and don't depend on machines of war to protect their living spaces or possessions can surely teach us something precious about life. They can show us how to bring our spirituality down to Earth and how to live harmoniously within the environment. They hold the remnants of our lost past that we must first recover, then protect and nurture. We need to walk down the path from which we came to discover where we made the wrong turn and then, carrying what we have learned, begin to walk a new path.

This is not to imply that we should all start living exactly as indigenous people do. What I'm suggesting is that we consider what would happen if instead of conquering and dismissing the worldview of the last remaining Nature-based communities, we would respect them and learn about the differences between their cultures and ours in order to better assess our current situation and the many steps necessary for our recovery.

In doing so, however, we should not imitate the spiritual practices, customs, or ways of life of native peoples. Each indigenous group has developed in a unique way that relates to the environment in which its people live and the life situations they have encountered in that place over time. Our place and our world today are far different from theirs. What we can do, though, is learn how to develop our relationship with Earth by incorporating their worldview into our own. Developing our own practices and traditions from the clues found in Nature-based cultures can also provide us with the determination so desperately needed to save these cultures from extinction. Too many beautiful and profound Earth-honoring cultures have already disappeared. I urge you to support the many organizations helping to preserve these last indigenous peoples.

At the same time, we should be careful not to disturb the delicate balance of such cultures through our help or influence. Participants in my workshops often ask if it is possible to walk with the indigenous people and shamans whose influences are responsible for the creation of many of these Earthwalks. Ironically, it is precisely their separation from the modern world that has allowed peoples like the Huichol to survive. The world's core indigenous communities most often live in extremely remote areas and are not easy to reach. If our contact with them or their sacred places is not carried out carefully and respectfully, mere contact easily becomes significant disruption.

Every day such people are being pushed into smaller areas. Every day their sacred places are being violated to the point that even they can't visit them anymore—a tragic circumstance that every indigenous group on our continent has had to deal with since the arrival of the first ships from Europe. Those people whom I know, love, and respect—my brothers and sisters of the mountains, the Huichol—live largely as they have for thousands of years. Unless we have been invited by a particular indigenous group, which is happening more as they see how sharing with us helps heal Earth, we should honor their solitude and isolation from our world.

The question of whether we can walk with them, however, can be considered from another point of view: We can walk with them every day of our lives by walking with the same Earth-honoring energy and intention in our hearts as they have in theirs; by walking with our animal relatives, the trees, and the nierikas; and of course by walking with each other. We can share these Earthwalks with the people we love—and even with those we may not even know. The magic of walking in Nature and the benefits of reconnecting with Earth are things we should all share.

I genuinely hope to meet you out walking someday, to enjoy with you a ray of sunshine and a breath of air, to walk together for a moment or a lifetime.

For information about future workshops, lectures, and activities, visit James Endredy's Web site at www.JamesEndredy.com. You can join his mailing list by sending a message to mailinglist@JamesEndredy.com